Journey Tools

Personal Workbook

Donny Godsey, Katy Pistole, and Robyn Henning

©2023 by Donny Godsey

Second Edition

All rights reserved. First printing 2020

Printed in the United States of America

No part of this publication may be reproduced, stored in a retrieval system, or transmitted in any form by any means – electronic, mechanical, digital, photocopying, recording or otherwise – without written permission from the publisher.

Unless otherwise indicated, all Scripture quotations are taken from the NEW AMERICAN STANDARD BIBLE®, Copyright ©1960, 1962, 1963, 1968, 1971, 1972, 1973, 1975, 1977, 1995 by The Lockman Foundation. Used with permission.

Compiled and edited by Robyn Henning and Katy Pistole

Contents

Welcome to the Journey Tools 7

Section One 9

Welcome - Video One 11

Journey Tools and Skills Overview - Video Two 12

How to use this Experience 13

Cautions and Expectations 14

The 'God Ask' Video 16

Section Two 18

Intro to the 7 Compasses 19

Read This! 20

Connecting with Jesus 21

God in Our "Now" 24

PLUTO 26

Receiving from the Lord and Partnering with Him 27

The Emotional Compass 29

Journaling Style #1—Release Method 33

Journaling Style #2—Diary Method 34

Behavioral Compass 35

Agenda Compass 36

Belief and Thinking Compass 37

Body Compass 39

Enemy Compass 40

Holy Spirit Compass 41

Questions about the Compasses 42

The Golden Question 43

Section Three – Shifting Resistance 44

ABC's of Fear, Anxiety, Depression and Worry 46

Miracles in No Man's Land 47

Deeper Dive Into Permissions 50

The Power of With 57

Blame 60

Section Four 63

Intro to the F.E.D. Map 64

Biblical Forgiveness 66

Biblical Exchange 68

Biblical Declaration 70

F.E.D. Map Purpose & Cautions 72

Walking Through the F.E.D. Map 76

The Power of Partnering 86

Unplugging from Shame 94

Section Five - Addiction and Idolatry 98

Building and Breaking Overview 99

Idols of the Heart: Problem 100

Idols of the Heart: Exchange 102

Idols of the Heart: 4 Zones 103

Idolatry & Betrayal 105

Building and Breaking Tools - Bonding with God 109

Building and Breaking Tools - P.U.T.T. 110

Section Six – Grief Healed 111

5 Stages of Grief and Recovery - Video 1 112

5 Stages of Grief & Recovery - Video 2 114

5 Stages of Grief & Recovery - Video 3 116

5 Stages of Grief & Recovery - Video 4 118

5 Stages of Grief & Recovery - Video 5 121

Complex Grief 123

Understanding and Healing Heartbreak 124

Section Seven 125

Relational Pathway Overview 126

Pathways and Walls 127

Trusting and Valuing God - Communication and Correction................................ 130

Trusting and Valuing God - Availability and Ownership 134

Trusting & Valuing God - Belonging & Identity - Timelines 137

Trusting and Valuing God – Two Trees 140

Trusting and Valuing God – Three Men (or Women) 142

Trusting and Valuing God- Healer Sanctifier.. 147

Trusting and Valuing God – Need Meeter and Jealous Lover 151

Trusting and Valuing God – Peacemaker 158

Trusting and Valuing God – Lion & Lamb 160

Trusting and Valuing God – Promise Keeper 162

Section Eight – Trusting and Valuing Others 165

Clover Tool 166

Clover Tool – Shift Mindset First 167

Clover Tool Walk Through 169

Trusting and Valuing Others – C&C Drop the Rope 171

Trusting and Valuing Others – C&C Identity Based Correction 172

Choose Your Path... 173

   PATH A: (Everyone) 173

Navigating Relationships in Abundance 173

Compass Intercessory Application 175

FED Map Intercessory Application 176

 PATH B: (For Healthy Marriages) 179

Trusting and Valuing Others – Emotionally 179

Trusting and Valuing Others – Finances 182

Trusting and Valuing Others – Roles 184

Trusting and Valuing Others – Spiritual Growth 186

Trusting and Valuing Others – Recreation 188

Trusting and Valuing Others – Physical and Sexual Intimacy 190

Journey Tools Wrap Up 192

Section Nine - Blank Forms/Resources* 193

Welcome to the Journey Tools

What is a journey, and why do I need to know that I am on a journey?

If I don't realize that I am on a journey, I will not recognize that I am lost. According to Scripture, I was born lost. Whether I am aware of it or not, my journey on earth began at my physical birth and will end when I get Home to Heaven. I am convinced that the purpose of my journey is to find The Source of love, joy and peace, and to live FROM that source. Jesus is the only perfect, eternal and abundant Source.

I don't know where you are on your journey, but we would love to walk with you awhile. Jesus is your compass, your map, your guide. He is your Protector and Provider. I don't know if you have ever thought about Him this way but I do know this. He is the One who knows you. He is sufficient to lead you into His perfect Peace and Abundant Life in this moment and the next.

Our heartbeat is to equip you with the foundational tools required to help you navigate this journey with the peace and joy that is yours by virtue of your new birth and identity in Jesus Christ.

We are honored to link arms and journey with you.

Thank you,
Donny Godsey and The Journey Tools Team

Prepare for the Journey!

Pray for understanding and protection. I suggest that participants recruit 5-10 people to pray for them, as well as this ministry in this season together. We all want deeper freedom and understanding. Keep your prayer support people engaged by updating them with snippets of what you learned or what God has done.

PRAY about finding a trusted person in our 1-to-1 network (if you should need that level of care to get unstuck) or consider one of our online group experiences that meet weekly. In one of our real world pilot groups, I gave participants the option to do the partner exercises and live practices in the group. They all politely refused. Near the end of the pilot, nearly all stated that they had wished I had made them do the practice partner exercises.

All care interactions in our network are online ONLY. Don't ever meet with someone in an unsafe way.

Take notes of both the material and what the Holy Spirit brings to mind as you watch the videos.

Ask questions for better discussion context. We love constructive feedback and want to make this a great experience for everyone.

Test drive. This is not a glass-case experience about theology or theory. This is an "invite God into your situation and see what He does".

Journal your experience and write everything down. God may show you something that will better empower you and all participants in your group. I promise that God will show you new things every time you ask Him.

Section One

Welcome—Video

Journey Tools and Skills Overview—Video

How to Use This Experience—Text

Expectations and Cautions—Text

The "God Ask" - Video

Welcome - Video One

How do you feel about beginning your journey with the upcoming tools?

_____
_____
_____
_____
_____
_____

But seek first the kingdom of God and his righteousness, and all these things will be added to you. Matthew 6:33 (ESV)

Journey Tools and Skills Overview - Video Two

The Seven Compasses—Our Now State

The F.E.D. Map—Forgiveness. Exchange. Declaration.

Building and Breaking Tools—How do Heartbreak and Addiction Correlate?

Relational Pathways—How do I Relate to God, Myself and Others?

As Donny described the overview of the course, did you experience any emotional reaction or response to the tools and your journey?

_____
_____
_____
_____
_____
_____
_____
_____
_____
_____
_____
_____

We can't wait to see what Jesus has for you!

How to use this Experience

All care interactions in our network are online ONLY. Don't ever meet with someone in an unsafe way.

Take notes of both the material and what the Holy Spirit brings to mind as you watch the videos.

Ask questions on here under related resources for better discussion context. We love constructive feedback and want to make this a better experience for everyone.

Test drive. This is not a glass-case experience about theology or theory. This is an "invite God into your situation and see what He does" experience.

Journal your experience and write down everything. God may show you something that will better empower all participants. Share only what you feel comfortable sharing.

If something doesn't make sense, please say so. Ask questions in the group under a related resource. Challenge it against what the Bible says.

Be courteous and kind. People here may be under a heavier load than you perceive or may have seen life from a very different viewpoint. God is their Maker, too, and He can lead them as they seek Him.

At the right time, ask God to bring the right people to you who may also need this prayer tool or equipping. It is eye-opening when you see it work with others! This over-all experience is intended to help, not harm, so be careful and use common sense.

If you are feeling led to harm to yourself, or others, or break some law, then stop and seek the level of professional help that is not offered here.

Cautions and Expectations

Welcome to the Journey Tools Training and Community. We will be moving daily through video lessons, optional partner exercises, and homework. By the end of the experience you will have a better handle on some very powerful prayer tools and hopefully the skills to use them well. At the same time, you are responsible for you and what actions you take in the group or outside of it. Please work under the authority of your local church leadership for wisdom, guidance, and boundaries

This experience is not intended to be an "end-all" solution for spiritual growth or a "one-size-fits-all" solution for certain situations. Even in the Gospel accounts, Jesus healed many problems in many ways, some not specific.

Also, the verses or concepts taught are open to interpretation and will be seen differently based on previous teachings people have been exposed to. Please seek the Lord by both His Word and His Spirit. Though we believe the Bible to be infallible, our own ability to correctly understand or interpret can change or even be situational, therefore, be gracious and kind to yourself and others.

Interact within your means and with the blessing of your local church body. We all appreciate prayer, but if you or someone else needs medical or professional help beyond your experience, credentials, and skills then know when to recognize that and refer them to seek additional help.

If God by His grace, does miracles for you or someone else, awesome! Give Him the credit and praise. This set of prayer tools were never meant to replace sound judgement, common sense, medical, clinical, or psychological professional expertise. It is also not intended to be a replacement for church life, Bible study, accountability, or other spiritual disciplines.

People working in an official capacity under the auspices of a church or ministry organization must by law report situations of abuse or intentions of harm to self or others.

This online experience is not "group therapy" so please do not disclose sensitive, personal information about yourself or others that may be seen by third parties you may not know or who may join the group later.

Please do not do self-promotion or cross promotion of other resources of any kind. The post will likely be deleted and the poster banned. This includes posting videos, external links, mentioning your business, church or group, unrelated prayer requests, or anything not directly related to Journey Tools.

This group is an educational resource and is not intended to rescue anyone from themselves or others. If you need immediate help, call your local emergency or authority numbers such as 911 or the **National Suicide Hotline 988**.

The 'God Ask' Video

How do you get 'stuck in your own head'?
_____
_____

Below, draw the arrows that illustrate a proper God Ask.

God

Me   Other

"Lord Jesus, what's the right question I need to ask _____?

"Lord Jesus, what's the right question I need to ask You?
_____
_____

How does a God Ask bring God into the middle of the conversation?
_____
_____

What is a Soul Ask?
_____
_____

When we use a Soul Ask, we are appealing only the person's _____, _____ and _____.

Even if it's a good idea, if it' is not _____ idea, it's a _____ idea.

Shadrach, Steve. *The God Ask: A Fresh Biblical Approach to Personal Support Raising.* (CCM Press, 2013)

Section Two

Intro to the 7 Compasses - Video

Read This! - Text

God in our "now" - Video

PLUTO - Video

Receiving from the Lord - Text

Emotional Compass - Video

Journaling Style #1 - Release Method - Video/Text

Journaling Style #2 - Diary Method - Video/Text

Behavioral Compass - Video

Agenda Compass - Video

Belief and Thinking Compass - Video

Body Compass - Video

Enemy Compass - Video

Holy Spirit Compass - Video

Questions about the Compasses - Text

Golden Question - Video

Journaling with the Golden Question - Text

Intro to the 7 Compasses

The 7 Compasses will dive into 7 areas of _____, explore the 7 roles of _____ and delve into 7 key _____.

All of these are important aspects of my _____ experience.

What is the primary purpose of the 7 Compass questions?

_____
_____
_____

Read This!

This content does not make you a counselor or a minister.

The materials are simply prayer tools to be used with yourself and others. Leave "advice giving" to the professionals. If you are not trained and qualified to do so, then don't give any life advice unless you want to invite potential *legal ramifications*.

I always let people know that I **do not give advice as** part of this ministry. I highly recommend doing the same unless that is exactly why they are coming to you as a professional. By the way, if you are using these tools correctly, then the person is getting their answers from the Lord by way of strategic questions in prayer.

Let God be the expert they connect with.

I say it all the time when meeting with others and they ask any advice based question, "That's a great question... let's ask God that question - He's the real expert in the room." I also let them know I am not the smartest person here nor do I know the best way to handle their situation. "We guess. God knows. Let's ask Him." is another favorite phrase I use. What are other ways to say that same thing? How would you invite someone to redirect their question to the Lord?

When we invite God in as the expert, amazing things happen that are beyond our own understanding.

Also, turning to His Word, letting them read it, and allowing the Spirit to speak to them that way also does wonders. "Check out Scripture XYZ and this one as well, what does it seem to be saying to you?" That process seems to honor the person and their learning process more than other ways I've seen Scripture used. The Socratic Method of using questions to teach gets people thinking through things and owning the right questions and answers.

Their authentic discovery > my proud display.

Connecting with Jesus

I love to ask this question. If I am not blown away by the magnificent presence of God, is because He is not present? Or is because I am not aware of His presence? What if God's deepest desire for me is that I would be so aware of His love, His sufficiency, His Life that everything else pales? What if that lovely song, "Turn your eyes upon Jesus, look full in His wonderful face, and the things of earth will grow strangely dim, in the light of His glory and grace …" is the choice I get to make in each moment? Every. Single. Moment.

I am convinced that God's deepest desire for His children is that we would come to know and live FROM His Abundant Life.

How do I connect with God? Through Jesus. His only begotten Son, the Last Adam, the First Fruit. Jesus sent His Spirit, the Comforter, to live in me and in every believer. Jesus drew us into His crucifixion and resurrection. He brought us into Himself. He is the Life. The only Source.

Jesus said to him, "I am the way, and the truth, and the life; no one comes to the Father but through Me. John 14:6

Why does God want me to live from His Abundant Life?

So I may experience freedom. Freedom from death and all its trappings. Sin and fear are just some of the fallout that comes from living under the law of sin and death. Jesus has broken the law of sin and death for us.

The Journey Tools are designed to equip every believer with simple but powerful tools to break out of the prison walls we may be feeling trapped in.

You have an enemy who hates you and is very good at twisting the truth.

The Journey Tools will help you connect with Jesus as He untwists the truth in you and for you.

Love, joy, peace, and the rest of the fruit of the Spirit are yours for the taking. Take them! Share them.

Join us in the Family Business of sharing His Life with a starving world.

Questions: Don't think about these too long, or try to answer the way you "should". Just answer with your first impression.

On a scale of 1 to 10, 1 being totally separated, 10 being completely connected, how close to Jesus do you feel.

        1   2   3   4   5   6   7   8   9   10

Now ask Him, "Lord Jesus, on a scale of 1 to 10, how connected are we?"

Write what He tells you

_____
_____
_____
_____
_____

Are you surprised?

_____
_____
_____
_____

Lord,
Is there anything else You want me to know about our connection?

_____
_____
_____
_____
_____

Mindset

Set your minds on things that are above, not on things that are on earth.
Colossians 3:2 (ESV)

What does it mean to "set your mind"?

The concept of setting your mind is similar to taking thoughts captive.

We are destroying speculations and every lofty thing raised up against the knowledge of God, and we are taking every thought captive to the obedience of Christ...
2 Corinthians 10:5 (NASB)

Where do thoughts originate?

There are several sources of thoughts. My beliefs, the Holy Spirit, and the enemy. My beliefs are crafted and influenced by experiences and circumstance. The Holy Spirit (who now dwells in me) can also influence me as can the enemy.

When I rely upon my experiences or circumstance or the enemy to influence me, I am "walking after the flesh" meaning that I am placing my confidence/faith/trust in myself, or others to influence me.

When I rely upon (place my confidence in, set my mind upon, have faith in) the Holy Spirit to influence me I am "walking in the Spirit".

I must choose where I place my confidence, where I focus my attention, who I allow to influence me. If I do not choose, I will default to flesh which is under the influence of the enemy. For many of us, the enemy's voice sounds clearer, more familiar and certainly more logical than the Spirit's.

God in Our "Now"

What is so important about my "now" experience?

_____
_____
_____

Now is the time where I

_____
_____
_____

You are not your _____

You are not an _____ you are experiencing an _____

What does scripture say about our now experience?

*For he says, "In a favorable time I listened to you, and in a day of salvation I have helped you." Behold, **now** is the favorable time; behold, **now** is the day of salvation.*
2 Corinthians 6:2

Why is it important to clear out the static or noise in my soul?

_____
_____

Is there something from your past or future that is affecting your now experience?

_____
_____
_____

What are you? Who are you? What determines your identity?

_____
_____

What is the primary goal of the enemy?

_____
_____

How is my now experience being tied down by the power of sin through the flesh?

_____
_____

So you also must consider yourselves dead to sin and alive to God in Christ Jesus. Let not sin therefore reign in your mortal body, to make you obey its passions. Do not present your members to sin as instruments for unrighteousness, but present yourselves to God as those who have been brought from death to life, and your members to God as instruments for righteousness. For sin will have no dominion over you, since you are not under law but under grace. Romans 6:11 –14 (ESV)

What is the primary fruit of walking in the Spirit?

_____

What is God's desire for you as His child?

_____
_____

Is this something you would like to participate in?

_____
_____
_____

PLUTO

What do the letters in PLUTO stand for? _____, _____, _____, _____, _____

Why is it important to listen and understand before moving on?
_____
_____

What is conversational prayer?
_____
_____

Has God shown you anything new, or have you experienced any "ah ha" moments?
_____
_____
_____
_____
_____
_____
_____

Lord, how can I make this truth a reality in my life?
_____
_____
_____
_____
_____
_____
_____
_____

Receiving from the Lord and Partnering with Him

The seven realities of experiencing God taken from Experiencing God: Knowing and Doing the Will of God (by Henry T. Blackaby & Claude V. King) [Bracketed comments by Donny Godsey]

1. God is always at work around you. [Pray and ask Him to reveal some of what that is.]

2. God pursues a continuing love relationship with you that is real and personal.

3. God invites you to become involved with Him in His work. [Partnering with God is something we will unpack more of through our time together.]

4. God speaks by the Holy Spirit, through the Bible, prayer, circumstances, and the church to reveal Himself, His purposes, and His ways. [God "speaks" is a commonly used expression for God communicating. Many times people will either hear the Spirit's leading, see visions of what He is communicating, or "just know" the truth of what to do or know by His Spirit - sometimes all three. During this time together we will be asking God fantastic questions. Don't let that get out of balance from other spiritual disciplines such as Bible study, prayer, and community - that is super important to keep in place.]

5. God's invitation for you to work with Him always leads you to a crisis of belief that requires faith and action. [Notice that word "always"? How about that word "crisis"? Look at this sentence word by word. When we partner with God to join Him in His work, it will require faith and action - wow! Exciting stuff.]

6. You must make major adjustments in your life to join God in what He is doing. [We will look at transitioning from point A to point B, evaluating our now experience along the way, and seeing what things we must let go of and what we get to receive instead. The second tool set in this experience is great for identifying what is keeping us from moving forward with Jesus. We will see a lot of adjustment in ourselves with that one and the third tool set helps us to adjust WITH God and others.]

7. You come to know God by experience as you obey Him and He accomplishes His work through you. [Our freedom and healing journey has a destination: to be more like Christ as we follow Jesus step by step. He is the focus. We use these first few journey tools to pull off anything that is holding us back.]

As a journal exercise, which one of these above seven statements stands out to you the most? Let's talk about that in the comments and share what the Lord shows us in the group call-in later in the week.

Thoughts

The Emotional Compass

For to us a child is born, to us a son is given;
and the government shall be upon his shoulder,
and his name shall be called
Wonderful Counselor, Mighty God,
Everlasting Father, Prince of Peace.
Isaiah 9:6 (ESV)

The compass tools are highly effective because they are simple ways to inquire of the Lord and get His understanding and insights very quickly. I enjoy seeing people react to how surprisingly powerful and simple they are.

It was like Spirit-led relational healing was hiding in plain sight all this time! The first step was to see it. The next step was to just do it. I have seen this work in seemingly minor issues as well as major, fresh grief cases, to old nagging pain such as 15-year-old grief issues. Jesus came through each and every time without fail!

All of the compass tools are based on three Biblical principles:
1. **Jesus is the Prince of Peace** - He is our source. (90% of the time peace is exactly what we or someone else was truly desiring during their time of need. He is our source. We are not going to find REAL peace anywhere else.)

2. *We have not because we ask not.* James 4:2,3 (Jesus loves invitations, but he is also a gentleman. I have not seen Him invade anyone's life, but He will wait on them to invite Him. He waits because He is honoring you and you are worth waiting for. He is the Lover of Your Soul. We are the Bride of Christ. This is part of His loving on us - the ones He redeemed. Oh, how He loves you! But we need to ask and with right motives.)

3. *Don't lean on your own understanding.* Proverbs 3:5 God's understanding is a gazillion times better and more complete than ours - period. Two things really help us not lean on our own understanding in using the compass tools.
   1) - ask the related questions out loud. It gets us out of our own heads and biased thinking.
   2) - once you hear a response, IMMEDIATELY go to the next question. Avoid processing each response till you have done at least three of the questions.

I'd like you all to learn about the first compass tool and then try it out to see how things go. It is always wise to pray for whomever is doing this to have courage. Please pray this with me, "Lord, bless me with the courage to truly hear from You. Bind up the enemy from messing with my trust in You and my willingness to be vulnerable to You. Holy Spirit, I welcome You to speak to me."

_____Compass

This compass processes how we _____, regardless if we know where that _____ was coming from or not.

1. Lord, _____ am I _____ right now?

_____
_____

Lord, _____ am I _____ that?

_____
_____

Lord, _____ do You want me to know about that?

_____
_____
_____

If complete peace and understanding comes upon you, then you are done for now, if not, then **repeat question #3** a few more times until you have the whole story. "Lord, what else do You want me to know about that? A nice auxiliary question at the end is "Lord, do I have all I need to know about that right now?"

After the exercise...

How was it? How did doing that feel? What new emotions came forth? Were they negative? Were they positive? Write them down. Ready for a bonus? Take that new emotion, positive or not, and run it through the process with that new feeling. "Lord, what am I feeling right now?... Why am I feeling that?... What else do you want me to know about that?" Any new insights from the Lord, write it down.

Some of you may be saying (or thinking), "But I didn't hear anything!"

That is ok. Really - it is ok. There are reasons for that and we cover those in a different section in much greater detail. You are my personal guest to relax and hang in there. The last thing I want is you to put pressure on yourself over that. Your prayer buddy does not need to force the issue either.

Common reasons for not hearing:

1. You are wired to do this more privately. Just ask, "Lord, do I need to do this later or in a different setting?" It is fine and that response may change over time.
2. You may feel like you have a foot on the gas and a foot on the brake. There could

be a number of reason for that. I found to best to ask, "Lord, is there anything holding me back from hearing Your voice or Your answer right now?" "Lord, if the time for this is good right now, would you please help me see that to get past that?"

3. "I'm afraid I'll hear many voices (again) and I don't like that." We cover that in much more detail in later sections. That issue can also flare up or not even be a factor depending on the subject, too. Just know that is will not be the case on every subject and it is beatable. Stay tuned!

4. Issues related to scary to talk to or abusive authority figures can impact relaxing with the Lord to hear from Him even when we want to. This is addressed in the next section. The question that gets that healing under way is, "Lord, who do I think of when I ask You these questions?" Write that name or names down. You are heading for real healing.

There are a few others but I'd like to address those later.
If at any point you feel overwhelmed or stirred up beyond what you can process on your own, reach out for ministry through your own church, small group, or our ministry network. We love you and want God's best for you - that includes emotional and relational healing.

On the next page is a list of emotions. I find these to be helpful when my soul is stirred up and I'm not sure what I'm experiencing. Add to the list to make it your own.

LONELY	ANGRY	AFRAID	SAD	HATEFUL	INADEQUATE	GUILTY
left out	furious	anxious	dejected	hostile	weak	ashamed
friendless	aggravated	frightened	unhappy	unfriendly	small	criticized
alone	distant	alarmed	dreary	mean	useless	cursed
forsaken	mad	jumpy	woeful	harsh	bashful	damned
lost	hard	fearful	sleepy	critical	meager	doomed
isolated	irritated	petrified	depressed	quarrelsome	deficient	dirty
withdrawn	frustrated	unnerved	miserable	nasty	powerless	judged
lonesome	boiling	tight	blue	jealous	vulnerable	condemned
insignificant	indignant	nervous	grieving	spiteful	defeated	embarrassed
separate	overwhelmed	timid	gloomy	resentful	stupid	trapped
rejected	cynical	shaky	glum	bitter	dumb	bad
unwanted	fed-up	scared	downcast	revengeful	worthless	punished
abandoned		terrified	heavy	hatred	inferior	
			shattered		incompetent	
					foolish	

BELONGING	PEACEFUL	HAPPY	SECURE	LOVING	POWERFUL	INNOCENT
popular	calm	joyful	safe	tender	strong	pardoned
famous	tranquil	ecstatic	protected	affectionate	energetic	pure
needed	quiet	cheerful	stable	warm	assertive	forgiven
important	serene	upbeat	optimistic	forgiving	upbeat	clean
well-known	collected	glad	sure	accepting	great	set free
influential	sedate	pleased	poised	kind	dominant	released
accepted	content	delighted	hopeful	devoted	pushy	exonerated
attached	composed	light	confident	loyal	assured	fresh
valuable	cool	bright	assured	sympathetic	sure	naïve
worthwhile	put together	vivacious	covered	caring	aggressive	acquitted
significant	relaxed	elated		free	confident	justified
worthy	organized	bouncy			superior	defended
		blissful			big	
					in control	

Journaling Style #1—Release Method

The Lord speaks to each one of us differently. Don't try to imitate someone else as you journal. Allow Him to guide you as you invite Him into the process of receiving.

Begin by taking an inventory of how you are feeling. There are no "right" or "wrong" answers. Allow yourself permission to be authentic with yourself and with the Lord.

Start at the top in whatever way works best for you.

Write out the first question, or simply fill in the workbook. Don't be afraid to get more paper or get a dedicated journal for this exercise.

1. Lord, what am I feeling right now?

_____
_____
_____

2. Lord, why am I feeling that?

_____
_____
_____

3. Lord, what else do you want me to know about that?

_____
_____
_____

Do you have any anxiety about His answers?

Write your questions down.

_____
_____
_____

You will know when you are done when you experience His peace. Rinse and repeat as needed!

Try this for 5 days straight and expect miracles.

We love you and can't wait to hear about how the Lord has met you.

Journaling Style #2—Diary Method

Quick Recap of the Emotional Compass before we dive into the Diary Method.

The three principles for the Emotional Compass.

1. Jesus is the Prince of Peace

2. *We have not because we ask not.* James 4:2,3

3. We are not to lean on our own understanding. Proverbs 3:5 Invite and receive God's perspective.

Instead of beginning with the three questions, write out your day with the significant events. After you have written what you want to write, go back through and ask the Lord to show you the red flags or emotional triggers.

This style may require more paper than we have allowed here. Just get more.

_____
_____
_____
_____
_____
_____
_____
_____
_____
_____
_____
_____
_____
_____
_____
_____
_____
_____
_____
_____
_____
_____
_____
_____

Behavioral Compass

And His name will be called Wonderful Counselor, Mighty God, Eternal Father, Prince of Peace. Isaiah 9:6

This compass processes what we _____, regardless if we know where that _____ was coming from or not.

Lord, _____ am I _____ right now?
_____
_____

Lord, _____ am I _____ that?
_____
_____

Lord, _____ do You want me to know about that?
_____
_____

If complete peace and understanding comes upon you, then you are done for now, if not, then **repeat question #3** a few more times until you have the whole story. Lord, what *else do You want me to know about that? A nice auxiliary question at the end is:*

"Lord, do I have all I need to know about that right now?"

_____
_____
_____
_____
_____
_____
_____
_____
_____
_____
_____
_____
_____
_____

Agenda Compass

God is our Master Strategist

He disarmed the rulers and authorities and put them to open shame, by triumphing over them in him. Colossians 2:15

This compass exposes what we _____, regardless if we know where that _____ was coming from or not.

Compass Questions

    1. Lord, _____ am I _____ right now?
    _____
    _____

    2. Lord, _____ am I _____ that?
    _____
    _____

    3. Lord, _____ do You want me to know about that?
    _____
    _____

If complete peace and understanding comes upon you, then you are done for now, if not, then **repeat question #3** a few more times until you have the whole story. Lord, what *else do You want me to know about that? A nice auxiliary question at the end is*

"Lord, do I have all I need to know about that right now?"

_____
_____
_____
_____
_____
_____
_____
_____
_____
_____

Belief and Thinking Compass

Lord, what am aligning my will to?

_____
_____

Here are the three principles for the Belief/Thinking Compass

1. Jesus is our Teacher
    My goal is that they may be encouraged in heart and united in love, so that they may have the full riches of complete understanding, in order that they may know the mystery of God, namely, Christ, in whom are hidden all the treasures of wisdom and knowledge. Colossians 2:2,3

2. *We have not because we ask not.* James 4:2,3

3. Don't lean on your own understanding.
    Trust in the LORD with all your heart and lean not on your own understanding; Proverbs 3:5

    Compass Questions

Lord, what am I _____ right now?
_____
_____

Lord, why am I _____ that?
_____
_____

Lord, is there anything else You want me to know about that?
_____
_____
_____

"For My thoughts are not your thoughts, nor are your ways My ways," declares the Lord.
Isaiah 55:8 (NASB)

But if any of you lacks wisdom, let him ask of God, who gives to all generously and without reproach, and it will be given to him. But he must ask in faith without any doubting, for the one who doubts is like the surf of the sea, driven and tossed by the wind. For that man ought not to expect that he will receive anything from the Lord, being a double-minded man, unstable in all his ways.
James 1:5 – 8 (NASB)

And do not be conformed to this world, but be transformed by the renewing of your mind, so that you may prove what the will of God is, that which is good and acceptable and perfect.
Romans 12:2 (NASB)

Lord, how can I use this Thinking /Belief Compass to partner with Your transformational power? I give You permission to transform my mind – my thoughts, and beliefs to conform with Yours.

_____
_____
_____
_____
_____
_____
_____
_____
_____
_____
_____
_____
_____

Body Compass

For You formed my inward parts; You wove me in my mother's womb. I will give thanks to You, for I am fearfully and wonderfully made; Wonderful are Your works, and my soul knows it very well. My frame was not hidden from You, when I was made in secret, and skillfully wrought in the depths of the earth; Your eyes have seen my unformed substance; and in Your book were all written the days that were ordained for me, when as yet there was not one of them. Psalm 139:13 -16 (NASB)

Or do you not know that your body is a temple of the Holy Spirit who is in you, whom you have from God, and that you are not your own? 1 Corinthians 6:19 (NASB)

Here are the three principles for the Body Compass

1. God is our Great Physician, our Healer.
2. *We have not because we ask not.* James 4:2,3
3. Don't lean on your own understanding.
   Trust in the LORD with all your heart and lean not on your own understanding; Proverbs 3:5

Body Compass Questions

Lord, what is my _____ doing right now?
_____
_____
_____

Lord, why is my body doing that?
_____
_____
_____

Lord, what else do You want me to know about my body?
_____
_____
_____

Enemy Compass

Hear, Lord, and be merciful to me; Lord, be my help. You turned my wailing into dancing; You removed my sackcloth and clothed me with joy, that my heart may sing Your praises and not be silent. Lord, my God, I will praise You forever. Psalm 30:10—12 (NIV)

The thief comes only to steal and kill and destroy; I have come that they may have life, and have it to the full. John 10:10 (NIV)

I love you, O LORD, my strength. The LORD is my rock and my fortress and my deliverer, my God, my rock, in whom I take refuge, my shield, and the horn of my salvation, my stronghold. I call upon the LORD, who is worthy to be praised, and I am saved from my enemies. Psalm 18:1 - 3 (NIV)

Here are the three principles for the Enemy Compass

1. God is my Rock, my Defender, my Victor.
   What, then, shall we say in response to these things? If God is for us, who can be against us? Romans 8:31

2. *We have not because we ask not.* James 4:2,3

3. Don't lean on your own understanding
   Trust in the LORD with all your heart and lean not on your own understanding; Proverbs 3:5

Enemy Compass Questions

Lord, what is _____ doing right now?
_____
_____

Lord, why is _____ doing that?
_____
_____

Lord, what else do you want me to know about that?
_____
_____

Holy Spirit Compass

But the Helper, the Holy Spirit, whom the Father will send in my name, he will teach you all things and bring to your remembrance all that I have said to you. John 14:26 (ESV)

The LORD is near to the brokenhearted ... Psalm 34:18 (NASB)

Here are the three principles

1. The Holy Spirit is our Comforter.

2. *We have not because we ask not.* James 4:2-3

3. *Lean not on your own understanding.* Proverbs 3:5

The three questions:

Lord, what are _____ doing right now?

_____
_____

Lord, why are _____ doing that?

_____
_____

Lord, what else do _____ want me to know about that?

_____
_____
_____
_____
_____
_____
_____
_____
_____
_____
_____
_____

Questions about the Compasses

Do you have any questions about the Seven Compasses and how to use them?

What Compass did you use the most?
_____

Was there a Compass that fit your personality more than others?
_____

Has the Lord surprised you with any of the tools yet?
_____
_____

How have the tools made a difference in harnessing what is happening in your "now" experience?
_____
_____

Journal these questions and share in the comments, or in your group.
_____
_____
_____
_____
_____
_____
_____
_____

Let God have the final word on what is happening in your life! He has this. He has you!

The Golden Question

This question rules over all the other tools and compasses, "Lord, what is the right question I need to ask You right now?"

Try using the Golden Question as a journal entry and see what He says.

_____
_____
_____
_____
_____
_____
_____
_____
_____
_____
_____
_____
_____
_____
_____
_____
_____
_____
_____
_____
_____
_____
_____
_____
_____
_____
_____
_____

Section Three – Shifting Resistance

Intro to Shifting Resistance

"ABC's" of Fear, Anxiety, Depression and Worry

Miracles in No Man's Land

Deeper Dive Into Permissions

Power of With

Blame

Intro to Shifting Resistance

Lord Jesus, where am I resisting partnering with You?

ABC's of Fear, Anxiety, Depression and Worry

For even when we came into Macedonia our flesh had no rest, but we were afflicted on every side: conflicts without, fears within. 6 But God, who comforts the depressed, comforted us by the coming of Titus; 2 Corinthians 7:5,6

†

Whoever confesses that Jesus is the Son of God, God abides in him, and he in God. 16 We have come to know and have believed the love which God has for us. God is love, and the one who abides in love abides in God, and God abides in him. 17 By this, love is perfected with us, so that we may have confidence in the day of judgment; because as He is, so also are we in this world. 1 John 4:15-18

Lord Jesus, is there anything I am relying on instead of You?

_____
_____
_____

Does the Lord bring anything to mind as you ask this?

_____
_____
_____
_____
_____
_____
_____
_____
_____
_____
_____
_____

Miracles in No Man's Land

Immediately He made the disciples get into the boat and go ahead of Him to the other side, while He sent the crowds away. After He had sent the crowds away, He went up on the mountain by Himself to pray; and when it was evening, He was there alone. But the boat was already a long distance from the land, battered by the waves; for the wind was contrary. And in the fourth watch of the night He came to them, walking on the sea. When the disciples saw Him walking on the sea, they were terrified, and said, "It is a ghost!" And they cried out in fear. But immediately Jesus spoke to them, saying, "Take courage, it is I; do not be afraid."

Peter said to Him, "Lord, if it is You, command me to come to You on the water." And He said, "Come!" And Peter got out of the boat, and walked on the water and came toward Jesus. But seeing the wind, he became frightened, and beginning to sink, he cried out, "Lord, save me!" Immediately Jesus stretched out His hand and took hold of him, and *said to him, "You of little faith, why did you doubt?" When they got into the boat, the wind stopped. And those who were in the boat worshiped Him, saying, "You are certainly God's Son!" Matthew 14:22-33 (NASB)

Have you ever partnered with God and felt yourself in "no man's land"?
_____
_____
_____

Do you feel like you are in "no man's land" right now?
_____
_____
_____
_____
_____
_____
_____
_____
_____

Wave Walkers

by Katy Pistole

I am a wave walker.

What is a wave walker?

A wave walker is someone who has abandoned the boat. A wave walker chooses to place her confidence in the Wave Maker.

As a wave walker, I don't need to make the waves. I cannot control the waves. I cannot overcome the waves.

A wave walker simply trusts the One who calls her out onto the waves.

A wave walker trusts Him, even when the waves look enormous. Even when they swamp the boat she has left behind. Even when the waves make no sense to her. Even when fear looks higher than the waves.

A wave walker trusts that even when she drowns, that He has overcome death.

A wave walker simply trusts Him, and steps from the boat.

I am a wave walker.

Will you join me?

Thoughts

Deeper Dive Into Permissions

How does Permission act as a doorway or blockage?

_____
_____

Anytime we encounter resistance, it indicates that there is a _____ issue.

Permission has to do with _____.

"His divine power has given us EVERYTHING we need for life and godliness through our knowledge of Him who called us by His own glory and goodness." 2 Peter 1:3 (emphasis added)

Jesus has given me His _____.

How does handling permission-based needs with rebellion play out?

_____
_____

Permission _____ fear.

"I am the gate; whoever enters through me will be saved. They will come in and go out, and find pasture. The thief comes only to steal and kill and destroy; I have come that they may have life, and have it to the full." John 10:9-10

How does getting permission open the door?

_____

Common Fear and Permission Issues:

1 Fear of _____.

2. Fear of _____.

How is blaming myself a false coping mechanism? _____

_____

"If any of you lacks wisdom, you should ask God, who gives generously to all without finding fault, and it will be given to you. But when you ask, you must believe and not doubt, because the one who doubts is like a wave of the sea, blown and tossed by the wind. That person should not expect to receive anything from the Lord. Such a person is double-minded and unstable in all they do." James 1:5-8

3. Fear of _____.

I don't have enough _____.

Lord Jesus, where is this fear of scarcity coming from?
_____

4. Fear of _____.

"There is no fear in love. But perfect love drives out fear, because fear has to do with punishment. The one who fears is not made perfect in love." I John 4:18

Lord Jesus, where is this fear of abandonment coming from?
_____

5. Fear of _____ with self and/or God.

Lord Jesus, how have I judged You or myself? _____

6. Fear of _____.

Control is an _____.

Lord Jesus, what am I afraid of if I yield control to You?

"Do not be anxious about anything, but in every situation, by prayer and petition, WITH THANKSGIVING, present your requests to God. And the peace of God, which transcends all understanding, will guard your hearts and your minds in Christ Jesus. Finally, brothers and sisters, whatever is true, whatever is noble, whatever is right, whatever is pure, whatever is lovely, whatever is admirable—if anything is excellent or praiseworthy— think about such things." Philippians 4:6-8 (emphasis added)

7. Fear of _____.

This is a _____ rejection of the possibility of a _____ me.

Being vulnerable that the new you will be rejected by _____.

"because greater is He who is in you than he who is in the world." 1 John 4:4b

Lord Jesus, who taught me to fear change? _____

Fear of change is a _____ question.

Lord Jesus, where is this fear of change coming from?
_____

Lord Jesus, what do I need to let go of to not fear change?
_____

"There is no fear in love. But perfect love drives out fear, because fear has to do with punishment. The one who fears is not made perfect [has not been fully embraced] in love." I John 4:18 (emphasis added)

"If you abide in Me, and My words abide in you, ask whatever you wish, and it WILL be done for you." John 15:7 (emphasis added)

8. Fear of becoming _____ or _____.

Sometimes God wants to increase our _____ as we depend on His strength.

Sometimes God wants to decrease our _____ so we depend on Him.

"For we are His workmanship, created in Christ Jesus for good works, which God prepared beforehand so that we would walk in them." Ephesians 2:10

"The Lord will accomplish what concerns me; Your faithfulness, Lord, is everlasting." Psalm 138:8

9. Fear of _____.

"Never take your own revenge, beloved, but leave room for the wrath of God, for it is written: "Vengeance is Mine, I will repay," says the Lord." Romans 12:19

Lord Jesus, how do I need to trust You with this offense?
_____

Lord Jesus, what am I missing out on by holding on to this debt/IOU?
_____

Lord Jesus, how is clinging to this debt costing me something?
_____

"So if the Son sets you free, you really will be free." John 8:36

"...for a man's anger does not bring about the righteousness of God." James 1:20

Lord Jesus, where is this anger coming from?
_____

"Be angry, and yet do not sin; do not let the sun go down on your anger," Ephesians 4:26

10. Fear of _____.

Lord Jesus, am I afraid my life will get harder if I do life Your way?
_____

Lord Jesus, is this true? _____

Lord Jesus, why is this true? _____
_____

Lord Jesus, what else do I need to know about this?
_____
_____

"Lord Jesus, I give myself permission and courage to receive from You and from my heart."

Lord Jesus, where do I lack permission for what I need right now?
_____

Lord Jesus, why is that?
_____
_____

Lord Jesus what else do You want me to know about that?
_____
_____
_____
_____
_____
_____
_____

Thoughts

The Power of With

What do you think about the idea that God does not need you to do things *for* Him, rather He wants to do life *with* you?

_____
_____
_____

What core need(s) got missed out on in a potentially good "with" moment?

_____
_____
_____

Why was your earthly father unable to meet all your needs?

_____
_____
_____

The heart of idolatry is hunger. I have a need that has not been met (or does not feel met). Can you identify a need that does not feel met?

_____
_____
_____

Do you know what you need? _____ Do you want what you need? _____

Humans were created with essential needs. My body NEEDS air, water and food. Without these elements, my body quickly (3 minutes for air) experiences death. My soul has essential needs also. These soul requirements are more urgent than air. My soul needs: unconditional love, acceptance, significance, identity, security and worth or value. Without a source for these needs, my soul experiences the fallout of death. The fallout of death is the opposite of the fruit of the Spirit. Love, joy, peace, patience, kindness, goodness, faithfulness, gentleness, and self-control are the answer for any wound, heartache, or hunger I may experience. My parents, siblings, friends, spouse, children are insufficient to meet these very real needs. Finally, my spirit needs just one thing. Life.

We will go deeper into how to connect with God as the all-sufficient source and Need Meeter for your human soul and spirit very soon.

"I am with you always, even to the end of the age." Matthew 28:20 (NASB)

What is the difference between "with" and "for"?
_____
_____
_____

Can you identify something you have lived for?
_____
_____
_____

Lord, have I been living *for* something (or someone) instead of **with** You?
_____
_____
_____

Fellowship, community and union are all a function of with.

*And looking upon them, Jesus said to them, "With men this is impossible, but **with** God all things are possible."* Matthew 19:26

How can God redeem your *with* experience?
_____
_____

Ask Him to show you how He wants to partner **with** you. Life. It's who He is. He is Abundant Life and He desires to share His Life **with** you!

Thoughts

Blame

We strongly encourage you to read Genesis 3:1-13:

Now the serpent was more cunning than any animal of the field which the LORD God had made. And he said to the woman, "Has God really said, 'You shall not eat from any tree of the garden'?" ²The woman said to the serpent, "From the fruit of the trees of the garden we may eat; ³but from the fruit of the tree which is in the middle of the garden, God has said, 'You shall not eat from it or touch it, or you will die.'" ⁴The serpent said to the woman, "You certainly will not die! ⁵For God knows that on the day you eat from it your eyes will be opened, and you will [a]become like God, knowing good and evil." ⁶When the woman saw that the tree was good for food, and that it was a delight to the eyes, and that the tree was desirable to make one wise, she took some of its fruit and ate; and she also gave some to her husband with her, and he ate. ⁷Then the eyes of both of them were opened, and they knew that they were naked; and they sewed fig leaves together and made themselves waist coverings. ⁸Now they heard the sound of the LORD God walking in the garden in the [b]cool of the day, and the man and his wife hid themselves from the presence of the LORD God among the trees of the garden. ⁹Then the LORD God called to the man, and said to him, "Where are you?" ¹⁰He said, "I heard the sound of You in the garden, and I was afraid because I was naked; so I hid myself." ¹¹And He said, "Who told you that you were naked? Have you eaten from the tree from which I commanded you not to eat?" ¹²The man said, "The woman whom You gave to be with me, she gave me some of the fruit of the tree, and I ate." ¹³Then the LORD God said to the woman, "What is this that you have done?" And the woman said, "The serpent deceived me, and I ate."

We are like God in that we desire _____.

Unlike God we are not designed to _____ good from evil.

How does the Accuser tempt you to judge God?

_____

The enemy is going to take our circumstances and tempt us to judge God based on our circumstances instead of judging circumstances based on God's Truth. The enemy wants us locked into a victim/revenge mentality. God wants us to freely forgive, allow the Blood of the Lamb to pay the debt, and then allow Him to convict the offender and (hopefully) lead to their repentance.

The Devil's Blame game involves enough _____ to sell it.

Lord Jesus, who or what have I judged?
_____
_____

Lord Jesus, have I judged You? _____

Others? _____

My Circumstances? _____

Myself? _____

Lord Jesus, how or what have I judged?
_____
_____

Lord Jesus, what have I judged about that? _____

- Actions
- Attitudes
- Slights
- Injuries
- Sinned against
- Abuse

Lord Jesus, why have I judged these in this way?

_____

Lord Jesus, what else do I need to know?

_____
_____
_____

Lord Jesus, how have I compensated in the wake of avoiding more pain and relational debt?

_____

Lord Jesus, what is holding on to this blame costing me?

_____
_____

Thoughts

Section Four

Intro to the F.E.D. Map

Biblical Forgiveness—Video

Biblical Exchange—Video

Biblical Declaration—Video

FED Purpose and Cautions—Video

FED Walk Through—Video

Power of Partnering—Video

Unplugging from Shame -- Video

Intro to the F.E.D. Map

This is a Biblical process that past clients have found to be effective at healing stubborn wounds and lies. In this process you will partner with Jesus as you learn a new way to put on and put off beliefs, behaviors or attitudes.

Why does it benefit me to solve my past pain?
_____
_____

What are the 6 issues covered by the F.E.D. Map? _____,
_____, _____,
_____, _____

F.E.D stands for _____, _____, and
_____

We will cover how to partner with Jesus in each section as well as show how to combine these sections together for a complete approach to resolving past and present issues of pain.

As a child of God, what is my primary purpose?
_____
_____
_____

The Combo Punch of Forgiveness, Exchange and Declaration helps me
_____
_____

As you consider doing business with God about past issues, especially forgiveness, do you have any fear? _____

Please know that fear is a normal and natural reaction to something new. You may be entering new territory in your relationship with God. Ask Him to provide you with the courage and persistence to wade through potentially difficult issues. You are not alone. The enemy would like to make you feel alone so he can tempt you to believe that you are uniquely broken; that not even God can love, rescue or enjoy being with you. It's a lie. You belong to the Good Shepherd. You are His problem, and you are not a problem for Him!

Lord Jesus, I trust You to be the Author and Finisher of my faith. I am willing to walk through deep and scary water with You as we, together, face the issues that have influenced and harmed me. Thank you for the healing that has occurred and will continue. I declare that I am Yours and You are mine

Thoughts

_____
_____
_____
_____
_____
_____
_____
_____
_____
_____
_____
_____
_____
_____
_____
_____
_____
_____
_____

Biblical Forgiveness

For freedom Christ has set us free; stand firm therefore, and do not submit again to a yoke of slavery. Galatians 5:1 (NASB)

Can you think of a time when you felt trapped by a past circumstance, person, behavior, or event?

_____
_____
_____

Then Peter came up and said to him, "Lord, how often will my brother sin against me, and I forgive him? As many as seven times?" Jesus said to him, "I do not say to you seven times, but seventy-seven times.

"Therefore the kingdom of heaven may be compared to a king who wished to settle accounts with his servants. When he began to settle, one was brought to him who owed him ten thousand talents. And since he could not pay, his master ordered him to be sold, with his wife and children and all that he had, and payment to be made. So the servant fell on his knees, imploring him, 'Have patience with me, and I will pay you everything.' And out of pity for him, the master of that servant released him and forgave him the debt. But when that same servant went out, he found one of his fellow servants who owed him a hundred denarii, and seizing him, he began to choke him, saying, 'Pay what you owe.' So his fellow servant fell down and pleaded with him, 'Have patience with me, and I will pay you.' He refused and went and put him in prison until he should pay the debt. When his fellow servants saw what had taken place, they were greatly distressed, and they went and reported to their master all that had taken place. Then his master summoned him and said to him, 'You wicked servant! I forgave you all that debt because you pleaded with me. And should not you have had mercy on your fellow servant, as I had mercy on you?' And in anger his master delivered him to the jailers, until he should pay all his debt. So also my heavenly Father will do to every one of you, if you do not forgive your brother from your heart." Matthew 18:21-35

How has this teaching shifted your perspective on forgiveness?

_____

What do you think about Donny's statement that the prison we wind up in is our own? The prison of unforgiveness is a bondage of the heart?

_____
_____
_____

Lord, is there someone or something we should explore in the F.E.D. Map?

_____
_____
_____

Thoughts

_____
_____
_____
_____
_____
_____
_____
_____
_____
_____
_____
_____
_____
_____
_____
_____

Biblical Exchange

Since, then, you have been raised with Christ, set your hearts on things above, where Christ is, seated at the right hand of God. Set your minds on things above, not on earthly things. For you died, and your life is now hidden with Christ in God. When Christ, who is your life, appears, then you also will appear with him in glory.

Put to death, therefore, whatever belongs to your earthly nature: sexual immorality, impurity, lust, evil desires and greed, which is idolatry. Because of these, the wrath of God is coming. You used to walk in these ways, in the life you once lived. But now you must also rid yourselves of all such things as these: anger, rage, malice, slander, and filthy language from your lips. Do not lie to each other, since you have taken off your old self with its practices and have put on the new self, which is being renewed in knowledge in the image of its Creator. Colossians 3:1-10

The concept of exchange is Biblical

Lord Jesus, if I give You _____, what would You give me in exchange?_____

Lord Jesus, what do I need to do to partner with You so that his exchange is a reality in my life?
_____
_____

Ask the Lord to reveal any unholy partners or patterns you may have inadvertently tied yourself to.
_____
_____

Why does God want you to be the initiator of the exchange?
_____
_____
_____

How has the concept of exchange shifted your paradigm, or pattern of thought about your behavior, belief or thoughts?

_____
_____
_____

Lord Jesus, how can I make this important concept of exchange part of my daily life?

_____
_____
_____

Thoughts

_____
_____
_____
_____
_____
_____
_____
_____
_____
_____
_____
_____
_____
_____
_____
_____

Biblical Declaration

Declaration is a form of _____,
_____ and an _____ to the spiritual world
around you. Declaration announces several things. Declaration is like a
_____ between two parties and it defines the roles and
expectations of both. Declaration signifies a new and active spiritual
_____ and agreement that replaces the old one that just got torn down.

Romans 6 (NASB)
What shall we say then? Are we to continue in sin so that grace may increase? May it never be! How shall we who died to sin still live in it? Or do you not know that all of us who have been baptized into Christ Jesus have been baptized into His death? Therefore we have been buried with Him through baptism into death, so that as Christ was raised from the dead through the glory of the Father, so we too might walk in newness of life. For if we have become united with Him in the likeness of His death, certainly we shall also be in the likeness of His resurrection, knowing this, that our old self was crucified with Him, in order that our body of sin might be done away with, so that we would no longer be slaves to sin; for he who has died is freed from sin.

Now if we have died with Christ, we believe that we shall also live with Him, knowing that Christ, having been raised from the dead, is never to die again; death no longer is master over Him. For the death that He died, He died to sin once for all; but the life that He lives, He lives to God. Even so consider yourselves to be dead to sin, but alive to God in Christ Jesus.

Therefore do not let sin reign in your mortal body so that you obey its lusts, and do not go on presenting the members of your body to sin as instruments of unrighteousness; but present yourselves to God as those alive from the dead, and your members as instruments of righteousness to God. For sin shall not be master over you, for you are not under law but under grace.

What then? Shall we sin because we are not under law but under grace? May it never be! Do you not know that when you present yourselves to someone as slaves for obedience, you are slaves of the one whom you obey, either of sin resulting in death, or of obedience resulting in righteousness? But thanks be to God that though you were slaves of sin, you became obedient from the heart to that form of teaching to which you were committed, and having been freed from sin, you became slaves of righteousness. I am speaking in human terms because of the weakness of your flesh. For just as you presented your members as slaves to impurity and to lawlessness, resulting in further lawlessness, so now present your members as slaves to righteousness, resulting in sanctification.

For when you were slaves of sin, you were free in regard to righteousness. Therefore what benefit were you then deriving from the things of which you are now ashamed? For the outcome of those things is death. But now having been freed from sin and enslaved to God, you derive your benefit, resulting in sanctification, and the outcome, eternal life. For the wages of sin is death, but the free gift of God is eternal life in Christ Jesus our Lord.

Thoughts

_____
_____
_____
_____
_____
_____
_____
_____
_____
_____
_____
_____
_____
_____
_____
_____
_____
_____
_____
_____
_____
_____

F.E.D. Map Purpose & Cautions

Forgiveness is Foundational to the Process

We have all been in a position where we need to forgive someone and also at some point will need to be forgiven for something we intentionally or unintentionally did to someone else.

Later we will cover how and when to confront someone's behavior as well as what to do if someone is not sorry, but for now let's look at how unforgiveness can keep us stuck and how to get unstuck.

Satan is the Father of Lies (John 8:44) and the Accuser of the Brethren (Rev 12:10). Those two go hand in hand. When we are wounded, whether great or small, the devil immediately hits us with lies and labeling accusations about ourselves, God, and others that are relationally toxic.

The devil wants us to adopt his perspective. Those lies and labels keep us in bondage. We are Children of God and are made for Truth.

Jesus said, *"I am the Truth."* (John 14:6)
The Truth heals us and sets us free. (John 8:32)
Jesus said, *"Whom the Son has set free is free indeed."* (John 8:35,36)
Living in abiding freedom is different from managing grudges, lies and labels.

We need release from those lies and labels we accepted about ourselves, God, and others. We receive release by partnering with Jesus' forgiveness and His Spirit speaking Truth to those lies, bringing His Light to those pockets of darkness and wounding. We get to exchange darkness for light, wounds for healing and self-effort for Jesus' Abundant resources.

Exchange is Pivotal and Essential in the Process

Exchange is not simply being rid of something but swapping it for the upgrade Jesus has already secured.

Often, when we need to forgive someone, we recognize the initial action and forgive it. Sometimes, though, we see that the issue returns to mind. So, we forgive again and again, or figure we stink at this forgiveness thing. This is actually God's grace, signaling deeper wounds that may be stuck below the surface.

Invite the Spirit to search your heart and address what needs to be exchanged. Then exchange it. We will cover this process in the F.E.D. Map walkthrough.

Declaration Secures and Completes the Process

Declaration is the third part. Declaration is part praise, part choosing to partner with the Lord in a state of yieldedness. Not only is it an extension of the exchange process, it is forsaking of self-effort and surrendering the God-sized job into the Lord's loving hands.

We will use the Deep Cleaning F.E.D. Map in your workbook. It is a combo-punch of Forgiveness, Exchange and Declaration interactions that helps you map issues with the Lord. We want to hear from Him for healing. We want to strategically ask the right questions and prayerfully respond as we "do business with God" in this life-changing process.

Getting the most out of the F.E.D. Map Tool

First, let's cover how to interact with the columns and rows. Each horizontal row in the chart has an exploration question paired with an exchange question per vertical column.

The following questions help uncover sabotaging beliefs and bondage issues. You may not need to fill in every slot. Ask the Lord the following questions to discover the areas that need attention.

OVERT ACTION: "Lord, what do I need to place before You for forgiveness?" You may have a line of events. Do each event separately.

DONE BY: Who was the main person or group? Who wounded you, sinned against you or offended you?

DIY vs DIW: "Lord, do you want me processing this on my own or with another person?" Write the name of the other person, if instructed.

WHEN TO PROCESS: The right environment and timing is important and can make a huge difference!

RATE THE PAIN: On a scale of 1 to 10, with 1 being no perceived pain, to 10 being off the charts, write the number you feel.

ABILITY TO FORGIVE: On a scale of 1 to 10, 1 being easy, 10 being impossible, how able are you to forgive this matter completely? Write the number you feel.

Partner with Jesus' forgiveness from the start.

Lord Jesus, I choose to partner with Your forgiveness that You have already given for _____(person) for _____ (action). I want to live in freedom, released from all lies and labels related to this person and action. Thank you, Jesus, for your death on the cross that paid for the sin of the world. This includes any sin done against me, by me or anyone else. I choose to walk in the freedom and peace of Your Truth. Thank you, Lord Jesus, for loving me first, and drawing me into Your Abundant Life.

You may need to unpack various related sub-actions until complete peace reigns in your soul. Experiential peace, pain and the Spirit's guiding are the indicators for repeating or not.

On the next pages we will walk through the map with all the rows and columns.

After the F.E.D. Map itself you will find detailed instructions for walking through it. It may seem complicated at first. Don't worry about filling out every block. The Holy Spirit will tell you which blocks you need to pay attention to. After you walk through the F.E.D. Map a couple times, your mind will become familiar with the pattern and it will not seem so difficult.

If your mind and soul resist the F.E.D. Map, walk through the Enemy Compass and the Holy Spirit Compass. Your enemy hates you and does NOT want you to forgive or find freedom.

Deep Cleaning FED Map

Overt Action/Event: _____ Done by: _____ DIY/DIW: _____

Rate the pain: _____ (1–10) When to Process _____ Ability to Forgive _____ (1-10)

	LIE	LABEL	TOOL/STRATEGY	VOW	NEEDS	EMOTIONS
Myself						
Exchange						
God						
Exchange						
Role of Offender						
Exchange						
Role of Recipient						
Exchange						
Action/Object Used						
Exchange						
Anything Else						
Exchange						

Walking Through the F.E.D. Map

Myself:

Lord Jesus, what lie did I believe about myself because (person) did, or is doing (action)? Or because of (event/circumstance)?

Lord Jesus, what is the Truth you want me to know about myself instead? Write your exchange answer in the gray block.

Lord Jesus, what label did I give myself because of this event?

Lord Jesus, who do You say I am? Write His exchange answer in the gray block below.

Lord Jesus, what tool or strategy did I pick up based on how I saw myself previously? Write your answer in the block.

Lord Jesus, what would You give me exchange for that if I gave that over to You? How do I need to partner with You so this is the reality in my life? Write the new tool or strategy in the gray block below TOOL/STRATEGY.

Lord Jesus, what vow(s) have I taken based on how I see myself in this context?

Lord Jesus, what would You give me in exchange for that vow if I let it go? How do I need to partner with You so that is the reality in my life?

Lord Jesus, what need was I trying to cover in my own strength because of that lie, strategy, or vow?

Lord Jesus, how do You want to be my Need Meeter for that instead? Write His answer in the gray exchange block.

Lord Jesus, what emotions did I experience as a result of this event?

Lord Jesus, I declare that You are my _____ and I am Your

Lord Jesus, I choose to partner with You and Your resources instead of what the enemy intended for me to take away from this event.

Have your emotions changed? Write the new emotion in the gray exchange block.

If you run out of room in any of the blocks, PLEASE journal about this. Your healing depends upon your participation in the process.

Thoughts

_____
_____
_____
_____
_____
_____
_____
_____
_____
_____
_____
_____
_____
_____
_____
_____
_____
_____
_____
_____
_____
_____
_____
_____

God:

Lord Jesus, what lie did I believe about You because of (person) doing (action)?

Lord Jesus, what is the Truth You want me to know about You instead? Write the Truth in the gray exchange block.

Lord Jesus, what label did I give You because of this circumstance?

Lord Jesus, how do I need to experience You? I welcome Your revelation in any way You choose for me.

Lord Jesus, what tool or strategy did I pick up based on how I previously saw You?

Lord Jesus, what would You give me in exchange for that if I released that to You? How do I need to partner with You so that Truth is a reality in my life?

Lord Jesus, what vows have I taken based on how I see You in this context?

Lord Jesus, what would You give me in exchange if I let that vow go? How do I need to partner with You so that Truth is a reality in my life?

Lord Jesus, what need was I trying to cover in my own strength, because of that lie, tool, strategy or vow?

Lord Jesus, how do You want to be my Need Meeter instead?

Lord Jesus, what emotion was I feeling in reaction to that circumstance or person?

Lord Jesus, I declare that You are my _____ and I am Your _____

Lord Jesus, I choose to partner with You and Your resources instead of what the enemy intended for me to take away from this event.

Have your emotions changed? Write the new emotion in the gray exchange block.

Offender:

Lord Jesus, what lie did I believe about (offender, that person or position) because of (person) doing (action)?

Lord Jesus, what is the Truth You want me to know about that person/circumstance instead? Write the Truth in the gray exchange block.

Lord Jesus, what label did I give them because of this circumstance?

Lord Jesus, I choose to release my perception and judgement of them or that role, and embrace Yours instead.

Lord Jesus, what tool or strategy did I pick up based on how I previously saw that person or role?

Lord Jesus, what would You give me in exchange for that if I released that to You? How do I need to partner with You so that Truth is a reality in my life?

Lord Jesus, what vows have I taken based on how I see that person/role in this context?

Lord Jesus, what would You give me in exchange if I let that vow go? How do I need to partner with You so that Truth is a reality in my life?

Lord Jesus, what need was I trying to cover in my own strength, because of that lie, tool, strategy, or vow?

Lord Jesus, how do You want to be my Need Meeter instead?

Lord Jesus, what emotion was I feeling in reaction to that circumstance or person?

Lord Jesus, I declare that You are my _____ and I am Your _____

Lord Jesus, I choose to partner with You and Your resources instead of what the enemy intended for me to take away from this event.

Have your emotions changed? Write the new emotion in the gray exchange block.

Recipient:

Sometimes I see something happen to someone else and I am traumatized. Watching a bully beat up another person, witnessing an accident, or watching a loved one die from disease, create wounds that must be healed in order for me to move in freedom. The recipient is the person who was bullied, in the accident, or died.

Lord Jesus, what lie did I believe about (recipient) because of (recipient) being (action)?

Lord Jesus, what is the Truth You want me to know about that person instead? Write the Truth in the gray exchange block.

Lord Jesus, what label did I give them because of this circumstance?

Lord Jesus, I choose to release my perception and judgement of them or that role, and embrace Yours instead.

Lord Jesus, what tool or strategy did I pick up based on how I previously saw that person or role?

Lord Jesus, what would You give me in exchange for that if I released that to You?

How do I need to partner with You so that Truth is a reality in my life?

Lord Jesus, what vows have I taken based on how I see that person/role in this context?

Lord Jesus, what would You give me in exchange if I let that vow go? How do I need to partner with You so that Truth is a reality in my life?

Lord Jesus, what need was I trying to cover in my own strength, because of that lie, tool, strategy, or vow?

Lord Jesus, how do You want to be my Need Meeter instead?

Lord Jesus, what emotion was I feeling in reaction to that circumstance or person?

Lord Jesus, I declare that You are my _____ and I am Your
_____

Lord Jesus, I choose to partner with You and Your resources instead of what the enemy intended for me to take away from this event.

Have your emotions changed? Write the new emotion in the gray exchange block.

Action/Object used:

Sometimes someone uses something to harm me. A belt used to whip me can create negative beliefs about a belt. A belt is a thing I use to hold up my pants. That is all. A belt has no power over me unless I believe a lie.

Or, I can believe that standing up for myself is dangerous because I did it once and got punished. Standing up for myself with healthy boundaries is a necessary action. Jesus does not want me to behave like a doormat or victim.

Lord Jesus, what lie did I believe about (action/object) because of (consequence/circumstance)?

Lord Jesus, what is the Truth You want me to know about that action/object instead? Write the Truth in the gray exchange block.

Lord Jesus, what label did I give the action/object because of this circumstance?

Lord Jesus, I choose to release my perception and judgement of that action/object and embrace Yours instead.

Lord Jesus, what tool or strategy did I pick up based on how I previously saw that action/object?

Lord Jesus, what would You give me in exchange for that if I released that to You? How do I need to partner with You so that Truth is a reality in my life?

Lord Jesus, what vows have I taken based on how I see that action/object in this context?

Lord Jesus, what would You give me in exchange if I let that vow go? How do I need to partner with You so that Truth is a reality in my life?

Lord Jesus, what need was I trying to cover in my own strength, because of that action/object?

Lord Jesus, how do You want to be my Need Meeter instead?

Lord Jesus, what emotion was I feeling in reaction to that action/object?

Lord Jesus, I declare that You are my _____ and I am Your _____

Lord Jesus, I choose to partner with You and Your resources instead of what the enemy intended for me to take away from this event.

Have your emotions changed? Write the new emotion in the gray exchange block.

Anything Else

Lord Jesus, is there anything I missed that You want me to know concerning this?

Final Check—Emotion Column:

After doing business with the Lord, using the F.E.D. Map, look over the whole chart allowing your heart and the Lord to direct your attention.

Are there any negative emotions or painful memories that get triggered as you look over the F.E.D. Map?

If so, use the Emotional Compass for each issue/emotion that arises.

Emotional Compass:

Lord Jesus, what am I feeling right now? _____

Lord Jesus, why am I feeling that? _____

Lord Jesus, is there anything else You want me to know about that?
_____

Repeat Question #3 until peace is upon you for this issue.

Coming Full Circle:

Re-rate your perceived pain on a scale of 1—10

      1 2 3 4 5 6 7 8 9 10

Write the new pain level at the top of the FED Map and circle it.
How does the new pain level compare with the original pain level?

Re-rate your ability to forgive this issue.

      1 2 3 4 5 6 7 8 9 10

How does that seem when compared to when you began the FED Map exercise?

Lord, is there anything that is getting in the way of my healing and forgiving? If so, please show me what I may be holding onto.

Thanksgiving and Praise:

If/when the Lord has freed you in this instance, or you are experiencing His peace in a fresh way, I encourage you to thank Him for this moment.

Do not lie to one another, since you laid aside the old self with its evil practices, 10 and have put on the new self who is being renewed to a true knowledge according to the image of the One who created him. Colossians 3:9,10

So this I say, and affirm together with the Lord, that you walk no longer just as the Gentiles also walk, in the futility of their mind, 18 being darkened in their understanding, excluded from the life of God because of the ignorance that is in them, because of the hardness of their heart; 19 and they, having become callous, have given themselves over to sensuality for the practice of every kind of impurity with greediness. 20 But you did not learn Christ in this way, 21 if indeed you have heard Him and have been taught in Him, just as truth is in Jesus, 22 that, in reference to your former manner of life, you lay aside the old self, which is being corrupted in accordance with the lusts of deceit, 23 and that you be renewed in the spirit of your mind, 24 and put on the new self, which in the likeness of God has been created in righteousness and holiness of the truth.
Ephesians 4:17-24

But I say, walk by the Spirit, and you will not gratify the desires of the flesh. For the desires of the flesh are against the Spirit, and the desires of the Spirit are against the flesh, for these are opposed to each other, to keep you from doing the things you want to do. But if you are led by the Spirit, you are not under the law. Now the works of the flesh are evident: sexual immorality, impurity, sensuality, idolatry, sorcery, enmity, strife, jealousy, fits of anger, rivalries, dissensions, divisions, envy, drunkenness, orgies, and things like these. I warn you, as I warned you before, that those who do such things will not inherit the kingdom of God. But the fruit of the Spirit is love, joy, peace, patience, kindness, goodness, faithfulness, gentleness, self-control; against such things there is no law. And those who belong to Christ Jesus have crucified the flesh with its passions and desires. If we live by the Spirit, let us also keep in step with the Spirit. Let us not become conceited, provoking one another, envying one another. Galatians 5:16-26

The Power of Partnering

I have included chapters 7 and 8 of Romans on the next page.

If I partner with something or someone other than Jesus, I might be self_____

How did God design people? We are _____ beings.

What are the three parts of man? _____, _____ and _____

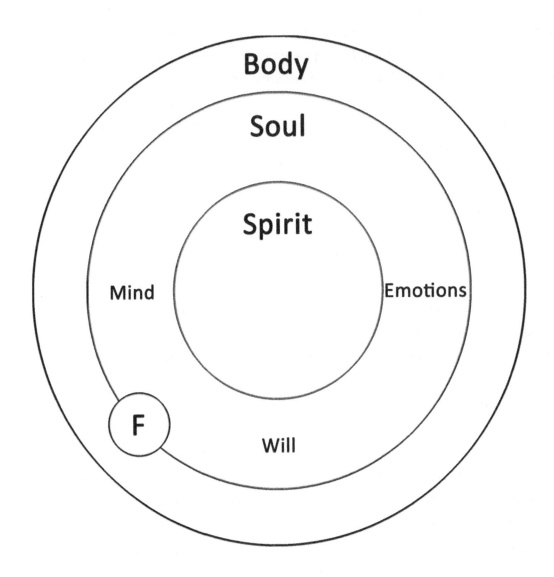

Where do our issues or hang-ups get revealed?
_____

Why?
_____
_____
_____

Where does my real (or true) identity come from? _____

The power of sin looks for places where I am _____ or
_____

Why does the power of sin do this?
_____
_____

Put off/put on are Biblical concepts for choosing where I will place my confidence, or where I look for my source or influence.

Romans 7 (NASB)

Or do you not know, brethren (for I am speaking to those who know the law), that the law has jurisdiction over a person as long as he lives? For the married woman is bound by law to her husband while he is living; but if her husband dies, she is released from the law concerning the husband. So then, if while her husband is living she is joined to another man, she shall be called an adulteress; but if her husband dies, she is free from the law, so that she is not an adulteress though she is joined to another man.

Therefore, my brethren, you also were made to die to the Law through the body of Christ, so that you might be joined to another, to Him who was raised from the dead, in order that we might bear fruit for God. For while we were in the flesh, the sinful passions, which were aroused by the Law, were at work in the members of our body to bear fruit for death. But now we have been released from the Law, having died to that by which we were bound, so that we serve in newness of the Spirit and not in oldness of the letter.

What shall we say then? Is the Law sin? May it never be! On the contrary, I would not have come to know sin except through the Law; for I would not have known about coveting if the Law had not said, "You shall not covet." But sin, taking opportunity through the commandment, produced in me coveting of every kind; for apart from the

Law sin is dead. I was once alive apart from the Law; but when the commandment came, sin became alive and I died; and this commandment, which was to result in life, proved to result in death for me; for sin, taking an opportunity through the commandment, deceived me and through it killed me. So then, the Law is holy, and the commandment is holy and righteous and good.

Therefore did that which is good become a cause of death for me? May it never be! Rather it was sin, in order that it might be shown to be sin by effecting my death through that which is good, so that through the commandment sin would become utterly sinful.

For we know that the Law is spiritual, but I am of flesh, sold into bondage to sin. For what I am doing, I do not understand; for I am not practicing what I would like to do, but I am doing the very thing I hate. But if I do the very thing I do not want to do, I agree with the Law, confessing that the Law is good. So now, no longer am I the one doing it, but sin which dwells in me. For I know that nothing good dwells in me, that is, in my flesh; for the willing is present in me, but the doing of the good is not. For the good that I want, I do not do, but I practice the very evil that I do not want. But if I am doing the very thing I do not want, I am no longer the one doing it, but sin which dwells in me.

I find then the principle that evil is present in me, the one who wants to do good. For I joyfully concur with the law of God in the inner man, but I see a different law in the members of my body, waging war against the law of my mind and making me a prisoner of the law of sin which is in my members. Wretched man that I am! Who will set me free from the body of this death? Thanks be to God through Jesus Christ our Lord! So then, on the one hand I myself with my mind am serving the law of God, but on the other, with my flesh the law of sin.

Romans 8

Therefore there is now no condemnation for those who are in Christ Jesus. For the law of the Spirit of life in Christ Jesus has set you free from the law of sin and of death. For what the Law could not do, weak as it was through the flesh, God did: sending His own Son in the likeness of sinful flesh and as an offering for sin, He condemned sin in the flesh, so that the requirement of the Law might be fulfilled in us, who do not walk according to the flesh but according to the Spirit. For those who are according to the flesh set their minds on the things of the flesh, but those who are according to the Spirit, the things of the Spirit. For the mind set on the flesh is death, but the mind set on the Spirit is life and peace, because the mind set on the flesh is hostile toward God; for it does not subject itself to the law of God, for it is not even able to do so, and those who are in the flesh cannot please God.

However, you are not in the flesh but in the Spirit, if indeed the Spirit of God dwells in you. But if anyone does not have the Spirit of Christ, he does not belong to Him. If Christ is in you, though the body is dead because of sin, yet the spirit is alive because of righteousness. But if the Spirit of Him who raised Jesus from the dead dwells in you, He who raised Christ Jesus from the dead will also give life to your mortal bodies through His Spirit who dwells in you.

So then, brethren, we are under obligation, not to the flesh, to live according to the flesh— for if you are living according to the flesh, you must die; but if by the Spirit you are putting to death the deeds of the body, you will live. For all who are being led by the Spirit of God, these are sons of God. For you have not received a spirit of slavery leading to fear again, but you have received a spirit of adoption as sons by which we cry out, "Abba! Father!" The Spirit Himself testifies with our spirit that we are children of God, and if children, heirs also, heirs of God and fellow heirs with Christ, if indeed we suffer with Him so that we may also be glorified with Him.

For I consider that the sufferings of this present time are not worthy to be compared with the glory that is to be revealed to us. For the anxious longing of the creation waits eagerly for the revealing of the sons of God. For the creation was subjected to futility, not willingly, but because of Him who subjected it, in hope that the creation itself also will be set free from its slavery to corruption into the freedom of the glory of the children of God. For we know that the whole creation groans and suffers the pains of childbirth together until now. And not only this, but also we ourselves, having the first fruits of the Spirit, even we ourselves groan within ourselves, waiting eagerly for our adoption as sons, the redemption of our body. For in hope we have been saved, but hope that is seen is not hope; for who hopes for what he already sees? But if we hope for what we do not see, with perseverance we wait eagerly for it.

In the same way the Spirit also helps our weakness; for we do not know how to pray as we should, but the Spirit Himself intercedes for us with groanings too deep for words; and He who searches the hearts knows what the mind of the Spirit is, because He intercedes for the saints according to the will of God.

And we know that God causes all things to work together for good to those who love God, to those who are called according to His purpose. For those whom He foreknew, He also predestined to become conformed to the image of His Son, so that He would be the firstborn among many brethren; and these whom He predestined, He also called; and these whom He called, He also justified; and these whom He justified, He also glorified.

What then shall we say to these things? If God is for us, who is against us? He who did not spare His own Son, but delivered Him over for us all, how will He not also with Him freely give us all things? Who will bring a charge against God's elect? God is the one who justifies; who is the one who condemns? Christ Jesus is He who died, yes, rather who was raised, who is at the right hand of God, who also intercedes for us. Who will separate us from the love of Christ? Will tribulation, or distress, or persecution, or famine, or nakedness, or peril, or sword? Just as it is written,

"For Your sake we are being put to death all day long; We were considered as sheep to be slaughtered."

But in all these things we overwhelmingly conquer through Him who loved us. For I am convinced that neither death, nor life, nor angels, nor principalities, nor things present, nor things to come, nor powers, nor height, nor depth, nor any other created thing, will be able to separate us from the love of God, which is in Christ Jesus our Lord

†

... in reference to your former manner of life, you lay aside the old self, which is being corrupted in accordance with the lusts of deceit, and that you be renewed in the spirit of your mind, and put on the new self, which in the likeness of God has been created in righteousness and holiness of the truth.

Ephesians 4:22-24 (NIV)

†

Therefore if you have been raised up with Christ, keep seeking the things above, where Christ is, seated at the right hand of God. Set your mind on the things above, not on the things that are on earth. For you have died and your life is hidden with Christ in God. When Christ, who is our life, is revealed, then you also will be revealed with Him in glory.

Therefore consider the members of your earthly body as dead to immorality, impurity, passion, evil desire, and greed, which amounts to idolatry. For it is because of these things that the wrath of God will come upon the sons of disobedience, and in them you also once walked, when you were living in them. But now you also, put them all aside: anger, wrath, malice, slander, and abusive speech from your mouth. Do not lie to one another, since you laid aside the old self with its evil practices, and have put on the new self who is being renewed to a true knowledge according to the image of the One who created him— a renewal in which there is no distinction between Greek and Jew, circumcised and uncircumcised, barbarian, Scythian, slave and freeman, but Christ is all, and in all.

So, as those who have been chosen of God, holy and beloved, put on a heart of compassion, kindness, humility, gentleness and patience; bearing with one another, and forgiving each other, whoever has a complaint against anyone; just as the Lord forgave you, so also should you. Beyond all these things put on love, which is the perfect bond of unity. Let the peace of Christ rule in your hearts, to which indeed you were called in one body; and be thankful. Let the word of Christ richly dwell within you, with all wisdom teaching and admonishing one another with psalms and hymns and spiritual songs, singing with thankfulness in your hearts to God. Whatever you do in word or deed, do all in the name of the Lord Jesus, giving thanks through Him to God the Father.
Colossians 3:1-17

Where do these "partnerships" come from?
_____
_____

Can you identify any partnerships you may have learned to utilize?
_____
_____

Partnering = _____

Spiritual agreements also _____with me.

God does not deliver you from your _____or your
_____.

God delivers you from your _____.

If/when I genuinely want to be delivered, or freed from a stronghold of flesh/behavior/belief/action/lie, there are certain steps to take.

Step 1

_____

Step 2
_____

Step 3
_____

Step 4
_____

Step 5
_____

Step 6
_____

Three Tips for Spiritual Warfare

Do you have a fleshly technique or tendency that you pull out for self-protection? Can you identify it?
_____
_____

Tip 1) Let go of
_____

Tip 2) If your conflict or problem is with another person, remember that your struggle is not
_____

Tip 3) If your conflict or problem is with yourself, remember that your struggle is not against
_____
_____

You were designed to _____ with _____

Lord, is there anything/anyone I need to unpartner with in my life?
_____
_____

How has this teaching about spiritual partnerships shifted your mindset on "strongholds" or other negative behavior you want to be free from?
_____
_____

Has this teaching shifted your ability to engage with the Lord in a different way?
_____

What are some practical ways you can engage what you have learned?
_____
_____

How can you plug in to relationship differently with God, yourself and others?
_____
_____
_____

Lord Jesus, is there anything you want to show me or teach me about unhealthy partnerships I may have engaged in?
_____
_____
_____
_____
_____
_____
_____

Are there any other thoughts the Lord is bringing to your mind?
_____
_____
_____
_____
_____
_____
_____

Unplugging from Shame

Where has shame been an issue in your life?
_____
_____

What was the real problem causing the lamp not to work?

Shame implies a _____ identity and we in turn embrace _____.
Lord Jesus, what lies have I believed because of shame?
_____
_____

Lord Jesus, what have I plugged into other than You to be my power source?
_____
_____

Lord Jesus, who shamed me and over what?
_____
_____

Lord Jesus, who taught me to shame myself?
_____
_____

What does Jesus do when we plug into Him?
_____
_____

"I am the vine, you are the branches; he who abides in Me and I in him, he bears much fruit, for apart from Me you can do nothing." John 15:5

Shame from their _____ that you ARE a _____ implies your behavior IS your _____.

"Therefore there is now no condemnation at all for those who are in Christ Jesus."
Romans 8:1

Lord Jesus, what false label do I still carry?

_____
_____

Lord Jesus, am I plugging in to You as my Source, or am I plugging into something or someone else?

_____
_____

Lord Jesus, how do I need to plug into You to function in union with You?

_____
_____

Lord Jesus, what self talk do I need to exchange with You?

_____
_____

Lord Jesus, how have I shamed others?

_____
_____

"Lord Jesus, I renounce using shame to correct others. I depend on You to speak Life to them through me instead (even when I am mad or hurt)."

_____
_____

Lord Jesus, how do You want to partner with me to encourage others?

_____
_____

Lord Jesus, who do I need to ask forgiveness from for shaming them?

_____
_____

Lord Jesus, do I have permission to let this light loose in my life?

_____
_____

Lord Jesus, do I have permission to be fully 'ON' with You?

_____
_____

Lord Jesus, am I trying to hide this light?

_____
_____

Lord Jesus, what permission do I believe I need (whether I realize it or not) to be fully free of shame and to partner with You fully for peace, power, and a sound mind?

_____
_____

Lord Jesus, why is that?
_____
_____

Lord Jesus, what else do You want me to know about that?

Thoughts

_____
_____
_____
_____
_____
_____
_____
_____
_____
_____
_____
_____
_____
_____
_____
_____
_____
_____
_____
_____

Section Five - Addiction and Idolatry

Building and Breaking Overview - Video

Idols of the Heart: Problem - Video

Idols of the Heart: Exchange - Video

Idols of the Heart: 4 Zones - Video

Idolatry and Betrayal - Video

Bonding with God - Video

P.U.T.T. - Video

Building and Breaking Overview

The Lord is near to the brokenhearted Psalm 34:18

He heals the brokenhearted and binds up their wounds. Psalm 147:3

What do you think about Donny's statement, "addiction is a form of misplaced worship"?

_____
_____
_____

Have you experienced grief? Are you currently struggling with grief?

_____
_____
_____

What are you most looking forward to in the Building and Breaking section?

_____
_____
_____

Lord Jesus,
Thank You for being our Healer, our Teacher and our Guide. Thank you for your perfect protection and provision. I trust You with my wounds, my pain and my grief. I can't wait to see how You use the Journey Tools in this next section.

_____
_____
_____
_____
_____
_____

Idols of the Heart: Problem

What do you think about Donny's statement that False gods = False Need Meeters ?
_____
_____
_____

Zone 1: Need-Meeter

Zone 2: Altar Supporting Thoughts, Actions, Habits

Conscious

Subconscious

God

Zone 4: Perceived Wall of Separation

Zone 3: Internal Well

Secret Pride, Unsurrendered Issues, Fear, Repressed Feelings, Shame, Guilt, Anger, Lies, Blame, Unforgiveness, Fall Out of Death Pain, Anxiety

What are the core needs of humanity?

Love is my primary need. Mankind was created to be loved, perfectly and eternally, by God. This is my primary purpose on the planet. Love is followed closely by acceptance, security, significance, value and identity. I must know who I am and what that means. I am either in Adam and spiritually dead or I am in Christ and spiritually alive.

What idols or addictions do you struggle with?
_____
_____

What actions, thoughts and/or habits (supporting behaviors) do you struggle with?
_____
_____
_____

Lord,

Thank You for being my Need-Meeter. You alone are the answer for the pain, grief, and bondage that I experience. You are my _____ and I am Your _____

What does the Lord bring to your mind as you see the Exchange illustration?

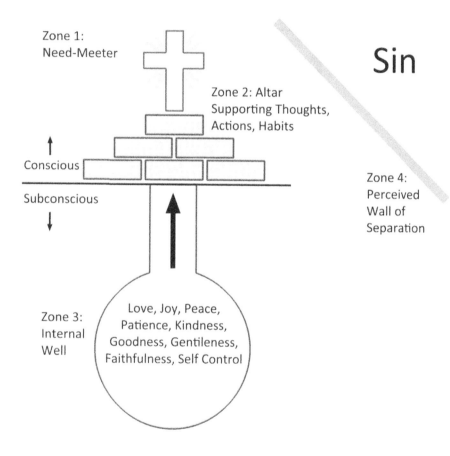

Idols of the Heart: Exchange

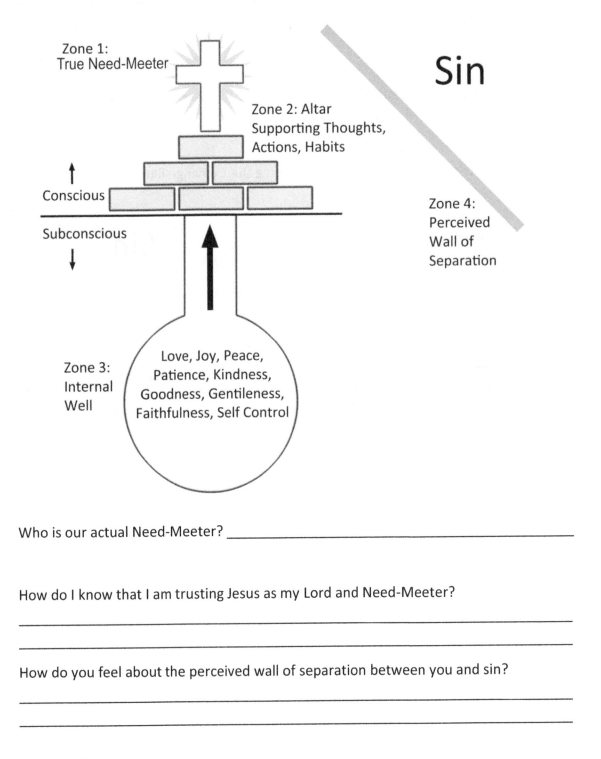

Who is our actual Need-Meeter? _____

How do I know that I am trusting Jesus as my Lord and Need-Meeter?
_____
_____

How do you feel about the perceived wall of separation between you and sin?
_____
_____

Idols of the Heart: 4 Zones

Zone 1: The place in my heart where either Jesus or addiction reigns.

Zone 2: The altar of worship, of thoughts, actions and habits that support what/Who I worship.

Zone 3: My subconscious, or what my life expresses.

Zone 4: The perceived wall of separation.

Zone 1: Need-Meeter

Zone 2: Altar Supporting Thoughts, Actions, Habits

Conscious

Subconscious

Zone 4: Perceived Wall of Separation

Zone 3: Internal Well

Where does the enemy focus his attack upon you?

_____
_____
_____

What is the BEST way to defeat the enemy?

_____
_____
_____

Who are the four people (or roles) you need in your life, especially if you are struggling with addiction?

_____
_____
_____
_____

Who are some folks in your life you can ask to plug into these slots?

_____
_____
_____

Lord Jesus,
Thank you for your perfect provision for me. Please show me the folks who can fill these important roles for me. Thank you for being my perfect provider.

_____
_____
_____
_____
_____

Idolatry & Betrayal

What does the Lord bring to mind when you think about betrayal?

_____
_____
_____

Jesus is interested in and committed to our healing. In what areas have you experienced betrayal? In what ways have you been the betrayer at times?

Part of healing includes owning my own "stuff" or taking responsibility for my side of things. Shame, guilt, fear, these are all part of being betrayed, and betraying others.

Betrayal assigns _____

See Matthew 6 on next page

What are the three things in Matthew 6? _____,
_____, _____

Does the Lord bring anything to mind when you think of treasure?

_____
_____
_____

The system Donny speaks of is designed to

_____
_____

The _____ speaks to the _____

What turns your head or captures your heart?
_____
_____

'I know your deeds, that you are neither cold nor hot; I wish that you were cold or hot. So because you are lukewarm, and neither hot nor cold, I will spit you out of My mouth. Because you say, "I am rich, and have become wealthy, and have need of nothing," and you do not know that you are wretched and miserable and poor and blind and naked, I advise you to buy from Me gold refined by fire so that you may become rich, and white garments so that you may clothe yourself, and that the shame of your nakedness will not be revealed; and eye salve to anoint your eyes so that you may see. Those whom I love, I reprove and discipline; therefore be zealous and repent. Revelation 3:15-19

Matthew 6

"Beware of practicing your righteousness before men to be noticed by them; otherwise you have no reward with your Father who is in heaven.

"So when you give to the poor, do not sound a trumpet before you, as the hypocrites do in the synagogues and in the streets, so that they may be honored by men. Truly I say to you, they have their reward in full. But when you give to the poor, do not let your left hand know what your right hand is doing, so that your giving will be in secret; and your Father who sees what is done in secret will reward you. "When you pray, you are not to be like the hypocrites; for they love to stand and pray in the synagogues and on the street corners so that they may be seen by men. Truly I say to you, they have their reward in full. But you, when you pray, go into your inner room, close your door and pray to your Father who is in secret, and your Father who sees what is done in secret will reward you.

"And when you are praying, do not use meaningless repetition as the Gentiles do, for they suppose that they will be heard for their many words. So do not be like them; for your Father knows what you need before you ask Him.

"Pray, then, in this way:

'Our Father who is in heaven, Hallowed be Your name. 'Your kingdom come. Your will be done, on earth as it is in heaven. 'Give us this day our daily bread. 'And forgive us our debts, as we also have forgiven our debtors. 'And do not lead us into temptation, but

deliver us from evil. For Yours is the kingdom and the power and the glory forever. Amen.'

For if you forgive others for their transgressions, your heavenly Father will also forgive you. But if you do not forgive others, then your Father will not forgive your transgressions.

"Whenever you fast, do not put on a gloomy face as the hypocrites do, for they neglect their appearance so that they will be noticed by men when they are fasting. Truly I say to you, they have their reward in full. But you, when you fast, anoint your head and wash your face so that your fasting will not be noticed by men, but by your Father who is in secret; and your Father who sees what is done in secret will reward you.

"Do not store up for yourselves treasures on earth, where moth and rust destroy, and where thieves break in and steal. But store up for yourselves treasures in heaven, where neither moth nor rust destroys, and where thieves do not break in or steal; for where your treasure is, there your heart will be also.

"The eye is the lamp of the body; so then if your eye is clear, your whole body will be full of light. But if your eye is bad, your whole body will be full of darkness. If then the light that is in you is darkness, how great is the darkness!

"No one can serve two masters; for either he will hate the one and love the other, or he will be devoted to one and despise the other. You cannot serve God and wealth.

"For this reason I say to you, do not be worried about your life, as to what you will eat or what you will drink; nor for your body, as to what you will put on. Is not life more than food, and the body more than clothing? Look at the birds of the air, that they do not sow, nor reap nor gather into barns, and yet your heavenly Father feeds them. Are you not worth much more than they? And who of you by being worried can add a single hour to his life? And why are you worried about clothing? Observe how the lilies of the field grow; they do not toil nor do they spin, yet I say to you that not even Solomon in all his glory clothed himself like one of these. But if God so clothes the grass of the field, which is alive today and tomorrow is thrown into the furnace, will He not much more clothe you? You of little faith! Do not worry then, saying, 'What will we eat?' or 'What will we drink?' or 'What will we wear for clothing?' For the Gentiles eagerly seek all these things; for your heavenly Father knows that you need all these things. But seek first His kingdom and His righteousness, and all these things will be added to you.

"So do not worry about tomorrow; for tomorrow will care for itself. Each day has enough

trouble of its own.

Lord Jesus, what idols do I have in my heart?

_____
_____
_____

Is there someone in your life who is struggling with an addiction? How has it affected you?

_____
_____
_____

If you are the person doing the betraying, you need to _____

If you are the one who has been betrayed, you need to _____

Use the F.E.D. Map and walk through the forgiveness process.

For if while we were enemies we were reconciled to God through the death of His Son, much more, having been reconciled, we shall be saved by His life.. Romans 5:10

Lord Jesus, I give You permission to sharpen my awareness about what turns my head. I want to partner with You as You reveal Yourself as my Need Meeter.

Lord Jesus, is there anything else You want me to know about idols, or addictions?

_____
_____
_____
_____
_____
_____
_____
_____
_____
_____

Building and Breaking Tools - Bonding with God

What did the Lord bring to mind as you observed the Nitrogen molecules?

_____
_____
_____

When molecules share bonds with each other, they also share energy. What have you bonded to that requires your energy?

_____
_____
_____

In what areas do you sense God that wants to share bonds with you?

_____
_____
_____

Lord Jesus,
Is there anything You would like me to know about bonding? How can I experience our bond more deeply? Is there something You would like me to cut bonds with?

_____
_____
_____
_____
_____
_____
_____
_____

Building and Breaking Tools - P.U.T.T.

Actually, then, it is already a defeat for you, that you have lawsuits with one another. Why not rather be wronged? Why not rather be defrauded? 1Corinthians 6:7 (NIV)

Therefore let us draw near with confidence to the throne of grace, so that we may receive mercy and find grace to help in time of need. Hebrews 4:16 (NIV)

Did the Lord bring anything to mind as you listened to Donny's story about the restaurant? What are your thoughts about bringing your petitions before the Lord rather than engaging in conflict with another person (especially a brother or sister in Christ)?

_____
_____
_____
_____
_____
_____
_____
_____
_____
_____
_____
_____
_____
_____
_____
_____
_____
_____
_____

Section Six – Grief Healed

5 Stages of Grief (1) - Video

5 Stages of Grief (2) - Video

5 Stages of Grief (3) - Video

5 Stages of Grief (4) - Video

5 Stages of Grief (5) - Video

Complex Grief - Video

Understanding and Healing Heartbreak - Video

5 Stages of Grief and Recovery - Video 1

5 Stages of Recovery & Life Transition

Stage:	Description:	Permission:	Crisis of:	Choice Between:
Denial	"There's no problem!" "What problem?" "Stop telling me I have a problem!"	To see and feel the problem	Reality	Insanity or Hope

Questions for Video 1

Lord Jesus, am I in denial about
_____
_____
_____
_____

Lord Jesus, give me the words to describe what I am denying
_____
_____
_____
_____

Lord Jesus, do I feel I have permission to _____
_____
_____
_____
_____

Lord Jesus, help me understand what this is a crisis of
_____
_____
_____
_____

Lord Jesus, give me Your clarity about my choices. I *want* to honor You, myself and others. How do I choose that? What does that choice look like?
_____
_____
_____

Lord, is there anything else You want me to know about this?
_____
_____
_____

5 Stages of Grief & Recovery - Video 2

5 Stages of Recovery & Life Transition

Stage:	Description:	Permission:	Crisis of:	Choice Between:
Denial	"There's no problem!" "What problem?" "Stop telling me I have a problem!"	To see and feel the problem	Reality	Insanity or Hope
Anger	Emotionally explosive or implosive blame	Forgive and let go	Judgement and Justice	Remaining burdened or feeling lighter

Questions for Video 2

Lord Jesus, is there someone I am angry with and blaming?

_____
_____
_____

Lord Jesus, do I have permission to forgive and let go?

_____
_____
_____

Lord Jesus, help me understand my choices and see my ability to partner with You and Your forgiveness. Is there anything else You want me to know about anger, blame and permission?

_____
_____
_____
_____
_____
_____
_____
_____
_____
_____
_____
_____

5 Stages of Grief & Recovery - Video 3

5 Stages of Recovery & Life Transition

Stage:	Description:	Permission:	Crisis of:	Choice Between:
Denial	"There's no problem!" "What problem?" "Stop telling me I have a problem!"	To see and feel the problem	Reality	Insanity or Hope
Anger	Emotionally explosive or implosive blame	Forgive and let go	Judgement and Justice	Remaining burdened or feeling lighter
Bargaining	Testing God, self and others (how close can I get w/o getting burned?)	Try Fail Succeed	Boundaries	Holding on the old patterns or mapping out new paths

Questions for Video 3

Lord Jesus, do I have permission to fail?
_____
_____
_____

Lord Jesus, do I have permission to succeed?
_____
_____
_____

Lord Jesus, do I fear failure or success?
_____
_____
_____

Lord Jesus, will it benefit me to seek help from a friend or counselor?
_____
_____
_____

Lord Jesus, help me understand and embrace healthy boundaries.
_____
_____
_____

Lord Jesus, help me see and walk in Your ways. I give You permission to show me dead or harmful patterns of thought, action, and belief that prevent me from walking in freedom. Is there something You would like me to know about my patterns of thought, action, or belief?
_____
_____
_____
_____

5 Stages of Grief & Recovery - Video 4

5 Stages of Recovery & Life Transition

Stage:	Description:	Permission:	Crisis of:	Choice Between:
Denial	"There's no problem!" "What problem?" "Stop telling me I have a problem!"	To see and feel the problem	Reality	Insanity or Hope
Anger	Emotionally explosive or implosive blame	Forgive and let go	Judgement and Justice	Remaining burdened or feeling lighter
Bargaining	Testing God, self and others (how close can I get w/o getting burned?)	Try Fail Succeed	Boundaries	Holding on the old patterns or mapping out new paths
Depression	Focused on circumstance, losses, external world, overwhelming pressure	Live without fear (financial, loved one,)	Worth Am I worth loving even if I can't ____? Are the false promises worth pursuing?	Giving in to external limits/labels of others or receiving God's limitless love

Questions for Video 4

Lord Jesus, do I have permission to live without fear?
_____
_____
_____

Lord Jesus, am I chasing false promises?
_____
_____
_____

Lord Jesus, am I worth loving? Even if I can't perform well?
_____
_____
_____

For even when we came into Macedonia our flesh had no rest, but we were afflicted on every side: conflicts without, fears within. 6 But God, who comforts the depressed, comforted us by the coming of Titus; 2 Corinthians 7:5-6

1 John 3 (NASB)

See how great a love the Father has bestowed on us, that we would be called children of God; and such we are. For this reason the world does not know us, because it did not know Him. Beloved, now we are children of God, and it has not appeared as yet what we will be. We know that when He appears, we will be like Him, because we will see Him just as He is. And everyone who has this hope fixed on Him purifies himself, just as He is pure.

Everyone who practices sin also practices lawlessness; and sin is lawlessness. You know that He appeared in order to take away sins; and in Him there is no sin. No one who abides in Him sins; no one who sins has seen Him or knows Him. Little children, make sure no one deceives you; the one who practices righteousness is righteous, just as He is righteous; the one who practices sin is of the devil; for the devil has sinned from the beginning. The Son of God appeared for this purpose, to destroy the works of the devil. No one who is born of God practices sin, because His seed abides in him; and he cannot sin, because he is born of God. By this the children of God and the children of the devil are obvious: anyone who does not practice righteousness is not of God, nor the one who does not love his brother.

For this is the message which you have heard from the beginning, that we should love one another; not as Cain, who was of the evil one and slew his brother. And for what reason did he slay him? Because his deeds were evil, and his brother's were righteous.

Do not be surprised, brethren, if the world hates you. We know that we have passed out of death into life, because we love the brethren. He who does not love abides in death. Everyone who hates his brother is a murderer; and you know that no murderer has eternal life abiding in him. We know love by this, that He laid down His life for us; and we ought to lay down our lives for the brethren. But whoever has the world's goods, and sees his brother in need and closes his heart against him, how does the love of God abide in him? Little children, let us not love with word or with tongue, but in deed and truth. We will know by this that we are of the truth, and will assure our heart before Him in whatever our heart condemns us; for God is greater than our heart and knows all things. Beloved, if our heart does not condemn us, we have confidence before God; and whatever we ask we receive from Him, because we keep His commandments and do the things that are pleasing in His sight.

This is His commandment, that we believe in the name of His Son Jesus Christ, and love one another, just as He commanded us. The one who keeps His commandments abides in Him, and He in him. We know by this that He abides in us, by the Spirit whom He has given us.

†

There is no fear in love; but perfect love casts out fear, because fear involves punishment, and the one who fears is not perfected in love. 1 John 4:18 (NASB)

Lord Jesus, help me receive Your limitless power and freedom. Is there something You would like me to know about this?

_____
_____
_____
_____

5 Stages of Grief & Recovery - Video 5

5 Stages of Recovery & Life Transition

Stage:	Description:	Permission:	Crisis of:	Choice Between:
Denial	"There's no problem!" "What problem?" "Stop telling me I have a problem!"	To see and feel the problem	Reality	Insanity or Hope
Anger	Emotionally explosive or implosive blame	Forgive and let go	Judgement and Justice	Remaining burdened or feeling lighter
Bargaining	Testing God, self and others (how close can I get w/o getting burned?)	Try Fail Succeed	Boundaries	Holding on the old patterns or mapping out new paths
Depression	Focused on circumstance, losses, external world, overwhelming pressure	Live without fear (financial, loved one,)	Worth Am I worth loving even if I can't ____? Are the false promises worth pursuing?	Giving in to external limits/labels of others or receiving God's limitless love
Acceptance	Authentic Peace	Accept the true nature of God, identity in Christ, ourselves, and our supply	Presence and peace	Playing games with who I am, listening to the enemy or remembering that God supplies ALL my need in Christ

Questions for Video 5

Lord Jesus, do I have permission to be the real me?
_____
_____
_____

Lord Jesus, do I feel fully present in the moment?
_____
_____
_____

And my God will supply all your needs according to His riches in glory in Christ Jesus. Philippians 4:19 (NASB)

Lord Jesus, is there anything else You want me to know about Your ability to supply my needs?
_____
_____
_____
_____

Lord Jesus, what can I do to make this Truth a reality in my life?
_____
_____
_____
_____
_____
_____
_____

Complex Grief

What did the Lord bring to your mind as you watched Donny explain Complex Grief?

_____
_____
_____

Lord Jesus, does this _____ bless my life?
                                    Addiction/habit/emotion

_____
_____
_____
_____
_____

Lord Jesus, is there anything else You want me to know about Complex Grief or loss?

_____
_____
_____

Lord Jesus, how can I partner with You to make healing a reality in my life?

_____
_____
_____
_____
_____

Understanding and Healing Heartbreak

What part of Donny's explanation of heartbreak resonates with you?
_____
_____
_____

Lord Jesus, when and how has my heart been broken?
_____
_____

The Spirit of the Lord God is upon me, because the Lord has anointed me to bring good news to the afflicted; He has sent me to bind up the brokenhearted, to proclaim liberty to captives and freedom to prisoners; Isaiah 61:1

Lord Jesus, what would You like me to know about my broken heart?
_____
_____
_____

Lord Jesus, what labels have I accepted because of my broken heart?
_____
_____
_____

Lord Jesus, what do You say is true about me?
_____
_____
_____
_____
_____

Section Seven

Relational Pathways Overview
Pathways and Walls
TVG - Communication and Correction
TVG - Availability and Ownership
TVG – Timelines
TVG - Two Trees
TVG - Three Men
TVG - Healer Sanctifier
TVG - Need Meeter
TVG - Peacemaker
TVG - Lion/Lamb
TVG - Promise Keeper

Relational Pathway Overview

We are made for
_____

"I and the Father are one." John 10:30 (NIV)

Lord Jesus, what would You like me to know about oneness with You?
_____
_____
_____

Lord Jesus, what would You like me to know about my relationship with others?
_____
_____
_____

Lord Jesus, what would You like me to know about my relationship with myself?
_____
_____
_____

Lord, is there anything else You would like me to know about my relational pathways?
_____
_____
_____
_____
_____
_____

Pathways and Walls

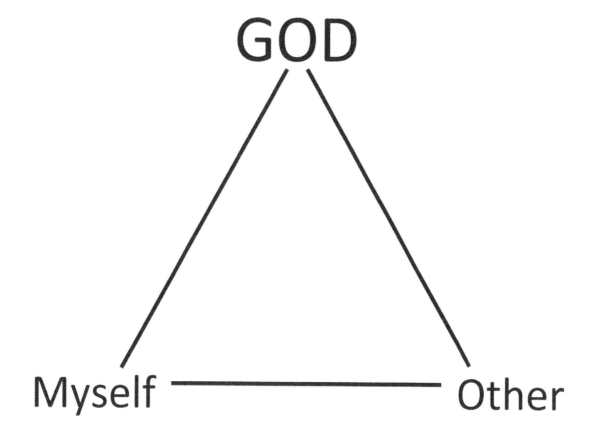

Do you find yourself in conversation in your head with _____?
(other)

Lord Jesus, what relationship do You want me mapping out now?
_____
_____
_____

How many pathways are there? _____

The Pathways are opportunities for _____ and _____ God and whoever you are in relationship.

What are the seven ways for trusting and valuing God?

1. _____
2. _____
3. _____
4. _____
5. _____
6. _____
7. _____

What are the seven ways for trusting and valuing others?

1. _____
2. _____
3. _____
4. _____
5. _____
6. _____
7. _____

Lord Jesus,
Please bring to mind anyone I may be harboring resentment or anger towards. I desire to walk in the freedom of forgiveness and healthy relationship with You, myself and others. Lord, I know that You are a gentleman and will not force me to comply with Your desire for me. I give you permission to bring to mind anyone who has harmed me in the present or past. I give You permission to walk me into a deeper healing and understanding of forgiveness. Lord, thank You for the gift of forgiveness and my ability to shed the burden of guilt for myself and others. Thank You for paying for the sin of the whole world. This includes my sin and anyone else's sin. This includes sin that has been perpetrated against me, by me, or someone else.
Lord Jesus, is there anything or anyone else You would like me to consider?

Lord Jesus,

I give You permission to show me blind spots, past wounds, or areas of pain that I may have stuffed or stifled. Thank You for being my safe place, my strong tower. Give me courage to partner with You in the process of healing.

<u>Thoughts</u>

Trusting and Valuing God - Communication and Correction

Have you ever been wounded by a person in authority? A parent? Teacher? Coach? Pastor or Priest?

_____
_____

How has past woundedness affected your confidence in receiving from the Lord?

_____
_____
_____

Lord Jesus, is there a gap between what I know about You and what I believe about You?

_____
_____
_____

But if any of you lacks wisdom, let him ask of God, who gives to all generously and without reproach, and it will be given to him. But he must ask in faith without any doubting, for the one who doubts is like the surf of the sea, driven and tossed by the wind. For that man ought not to expect that he will receive anything from the Lord, being a double-minded man, unstable in all his ways. James 1: 5-8

Lord Jesus, am I asking for Your instruction or Your opinion?

_____
_____
_____

What do you think about Donny's statement that "hearing God's voice as opinion only makes a statement that we are free moral agents open to other opinions."?

_____
_____

Lord Jesus, I pre-commit that I will obey Your instructions, not just seek Your opinion. Lord, I declare that You are my _____ and I am Your _____
Thoughts:

_____
_____
_____

What do you think about Donny's assertion that communicating with God is something we are instructed to do in scripture?

_____
_____
_____

Have you had any issues with hearing from the Lord?

_____
_____
_____

And without faith it is impossible to please Him, for he who comes to God must believe that He is and that He is a rewarder of those who seek Him. Hebrews 11:6 (NASB)

†

I will instruct you and teach you in the way which you should go; I will counsel you with My eye upon you. Do not be as the horse or as the mule which have no understanding, Whose trappings include bit and bridle to hold them in check, otherwise they will not come near to you. Psalm 32:8,9 (NASB)

†

For the eyes of the Lord move to and fro throughout the earth that He may strongly support those whose heart is completely His. (NASB) 2 Chronicles 16:9

What do you think about Donny's statement "if *it* (wounding that created fear of authority) had an origin, that means it can be healed"?

_____
_____
_____

Do you think the "it" could apply to other's wounds? If ANY wound (the source of misbelief) has an origin, it can be healed. Does this statement sound true?

_____
_____
_____

Lord Jesus, do I see You rightly?

_____
_____

Lord, do I have trouble trusting You for communication and correction?

_____
_____

Lord Jesus, do I feel like I need to figure it all out myself and operate on autopilot?

_____
_____
_____

Lord, do I have any authority figures I need to forgive so I can enjoy You fully?

_____
_____
_____

Lord Jesus, is there any defensiveness or aggressiveness, or any "ouch" still attached to any person or event in my past with respect to authority figures?

_____
_____
_____

Lord, is pride an issue in my heart right now?

_____
_____
_____

Lord Jesus, is there anything I am trying to prove to authority figures in my life?

_____
_____
_____

Lord, am I at ease with all authority figures in my life, or only certain perfect ones that live up to my expectations?

_____
_____
_____

Lord Jesus, is there anything else You want me to know about You, authority figures, or anything else that may need healing? I want to align myself to Your Truth, Your Word, Your Self.

_____
_____
_____
_____
_____
_____

Trusting and Valuing God - Availability and Ownership

I have been crucified with Christ; and it is no longer I who live, but Christ lives in me; and the life which I now live in the flesh I live by faith in the Son of God, who loved me and gave Himself up for me. Galatians 2:20 (NASB)

†

For whoever wishes to save his life (psueke) will lose it; but whoever loses his life (psueke) for My sake will find it (Zoe). Matthew 16:25 (NASB) Greek added in parenthesis

†

That day Jesus went out of the house and was sitting by the sea. And large crowds gathered to Him, so He got into a boat and sat down, and the whole crowd was standing on the beach.

And He spoke many things to them in parables, saying, "Behold, the sower went out to sow; and as he sowed, some seeds fell beside the road, and the birds came and ate them up. Others fell on the rocky places, where they did not have much soil; and immediately they sprang up, because they had no depth of soil. But when the sun had risen, they were scorched; and because they had no root, they withered away. Others fell among the thorns, and the thorns came up and choked them out. And others fell on the good soil and *yielded a crop, some a hundredfold, some sixty, and some thirty. He who has ears, let him hear."

And the disciples came and said to Him, "Why do You speak to them in parables?" Jesus answered them, "To you it has been granted to know the mysteries of the kingdom of heaven, but to them it has not been granted. For whoever has, to him more shall be given, and he will have an abundance; but whoever does not have, even what he has shall be taken away from him. Therefore I speak to them in parables; because while seeing they do not see, and while hearing they do not hear, nor do they understand. In their case the prophecy of Isaiah is being fulfilled, which says,

'You will keep on hearing, but will not understand; you will keep on seeing, but will not perceive; for the heart of this people has become dull, with their ears they scarcely hear, and they have closed their eyes, otherwise they would see with their eyes, hear with

their ears, and understand with their heart and return,

And I would heal them.'

But blessed are your eyes, because they see; and your ears, because they hear. For truly I say to you that many prophets and righteous men desired to see what you see, and did not see it, and to hear what you hear, and did not hear it.

"Hear then the parable of the sower. When anyone hears the word of the kingdom and does not understand it, the evil one comes and snatches away what has been sown in his heart. This is the one on whom seed was sown beside the road. The one on whom seed was sown on the rocky places, this is the man who hears the word and immediately receives it with joy; yet he has no firm root in himself, but is only temporary, and when affliction or persecution arises because of the word, immediately he falls away. And the one on whom seed was sown among the thorns, this is the man who hears the word, and the worry of the world and the deceitfulness of wealth choke the word, and it becomes unfruitful. And the one on whom seed was sown on the good soil, this is the man who hears the word and understands it; who indeed bears fruit and brings forth, some a hundredfold, some sixty, and some thirty." Matthew 13:1-23

Lord Jesus, am I truly available to You, or am I clinging to my (old, dead) life in some way?

_____
_____
_____

Lord Jesus, is there something in the way of me responding to You rightly?

_____
_____
_____

Lord Jesus, search my heart so I can do business with You.

_____

Lord Jesus, is this _____ getting in the way of Your best for me?

_____

P_____

L_____

U_____

T_____

O_____

You can find the PLUTO video (if you would like to watch again) in the Seven Compasses Section

Lord Jesus, what can I do to partner with You, Your Life and Love, to make this Truth a reality in my life?

_____
_____
_____
_____
_____
_____
_____
_____

Lord, what else do You want me to know about this?

_____
_____
_____
_____
_____
_____
_____
_____
_____
_____

Trusting & Valuing God - Belonging & Identity - Timelines

I have been crucified with Christ; and it is no longer I who live, but Christ lives in me; and the life which I now live in the flesh I live by faith in the Son of God, who loved me and gave Himself up for me. Galatians 2:20

†

Or do you not know that all of us who have been baptized into Christ Jesus have been baptized into His death? Therefore we have been buried with Him through baptism into death, so that as Christ was raised from the dead through the glory of the Father, so we too might walk in newness of life. For if we have become united with Him in the likeness of His death, certainly we shall also be in the likeness of His resurrection, knowing this, that our old self was crucified with Him, in order that our body of sin might be done away with, so that we would no longer be slaves to sin; for he who has died is freed from sin.

Now if we have died with Christ, we believe that we shall also live with Him, knowing that Christ, having been raised from the dead, is never to die again; death no longer is master over Him. For the death that He died, He died to sin once for all; but the life that He lives, He lives to God. Even so consider yourselves to be dead to sin, but alive to God in Christ Jesus. Romans 6:3-11

Jesus came to give us _____

*The thief comes only to steal and kill and destroy; I came that they may have life, and have it **abundantly**.* John 10:10

Jesus took all of our _____ so that we may be His righteousness.

Why do we often feel we don't deserve the gift of Jesus?
_____
_____
_____

For by grace you have been saved through faith; and that not of yourselves, it is the gift of God; not as a result of works, so that no one may boast. Ephesians 2:8,9

†

...even when we were dead in our transgressions, made us alive together with Christ (by grace you have been saved), and raised us up with Him, and seated us with Him in the heavenly places in Christ Jesus, so that in the ages to come He might show the surpassing riches of His grace in kindness toward us in Christ Jesus. Ephesians 2:5 -7

How is it possible that we can be both seated in the heavenly places WHILE still here on earth?

_____
_____
_____

What did Jesus do with your past?

_____
_____
_____

When you consider the Truth that Jesus exchanged your old life for His new Life, present, future and PAST, what happens in your soul?

_____
_____
_____

Are you holding your past against you?

_____
_____
_____

Lord Jesus, help me understand (to the best of my ability with my human, time-bound, eyes) this mind-blowing Truth that You have exchanged my old, dead life for Your

Eternal, Abundant Life. Help me partner with this Truth in my now, and forever.

Thoughts

_____
_____
_____
_____
_____
_____
_____
_____
_____
_____
_____
_____
_____
_____
_____
_____
_____
_____
_____
_____
_____
_____
_____
_____
_____
_____
_____
_____

Trusting and Valuing God – Two Trees

What were the two eternally significant trees in the Garden of Eden?

_____
_____

After Adam and Woman ate from the Tree of the Knowledge of Good and Evil, what happened?

_____
_____
_____

What do you think about Donny's assertion that Law = Death? Have you ever heard that before?

_____
_____
_____

... holding to a form of godliness, although they have denied its power; Avoid such men as these. 2 Timothy 3:5

†

There is a way which seems right to a man, but its end is the way of death. Proverbs 14:12

What did you think about Donny's request to take the heads or the tails of the coin?

_____
_____

What do you think about the statement that the battle is not against good and evil, but against Life and Death?

_____

How does your striving lead to frustration?

_____
_____
_____

What is the key to ending your striving?

_____
_____
_____

Lord Jesus, please help me understand this new way of living. This way that focuses upon *You* as the source of my right-ness (righteousness), not my choosing the "good' side of the Tree of the Knowledge of Good and Evil. Lord, please remove any blind spots and reveal where I am living from flesh (especially good looking flesh) rather than depending upon You.

_____
_____
_____
_____
_____
_____
_____
_____
_____
_____
_____
_____
_____
_____
_____
_____
_____
_____

Trusting and Valuing God – Three Men (or Women)

I have been crucified with Christ; and it is no longer I who live, but Christ lives in me; and the life which I now live in the flesh I live by faith in the Son of God, who loved me and gave Himself up for me. Galatians 2:20

Do dead people struggle with _____?

Do dead people sin? _____

Where does sin come from? _____

The power of sin is trying to keep you from aligning yourself fully with the understanding of who you are in _____

Why doesn't the enemy want you unleashed?
_____
_____
_____

What is the flesh really good at?
_____
_____

What happened to the messages of your old life?
_____
_____

What is true about you? Are you royalty?
_____
_____

What is the answer for the firing the imposter?
_____
_____

We demolish arguments and every pretension that sets itself up against the knowledge of God, and we take captive every thought to make it obedient to Christ.
2 Corinthians 10:5 (NIV)

†

Have this mind among yourselves, which is yours in Christ Jesus, Philippians 2:5 (ESV)

The Power of Sin talks to you in first person pronouns, sounding like your own thoughts. It seeks tempt, accuse and deceive.

What do you think about Donny's assertion that you can choose to partner with sin, or partner with Jesus?
_____
_____

Romans 6:1-14

What shall we say then? Are we to continue in sin so that grace may increase? May it never be! How shall we who died to sin still live in it? Or do you not know that all of us who have been baptized into Christ Jesus have been baptized into His death? Therefore we have been buried with Him through baptism into death, so that as Christ was raised from the dead through the glory of the Father, so we too might walk in newness of life. For if we have become united with Him in the likeness of His death, certainly we shall also be in the likeness of His resurrection, knowing this, that our old self was crucified with Him, in order that our body of sin might be done away with, so that we would no longer be slaves to sin; for he who has died is freed from sin.

Now if we have died with Christ, we believe that we shall also live with Him, knowing that Christ, having been raised from the dead, is never to die again; death no longer is master over Him. For the death that He died, He died to sin once for all; but the life that He lives, He lives to God. Even so consider yourselves to be dead to sin, but alive to God in Christ Jesus.

Therefore do not let sin reign in your mortal body so that you obey its lusts, and do not go on presenting the members of your body to sin as instruments of unrighteousness; but present yourselves to God as those alive from the dead, and your members as instruments of righteousness to God. For sin shall not be master over you, for you are not under law but under grace.

What do you think about Donny's statement that "you don't have a sin problem, you have a misalignment problem."?

_____
_____
_____

How do you feel about the concept that you are holy? Royalty?

_____
_____

seeing that His divine power has granted to us everything pertaining to life and godliness, through the true knowledge of Him who called us by His own glory and excellence.
2 Peter 1:3

We approach God by how we see Him, and by how we see ourselves.

We either _____ in who we really are OR _____ who we are trying NOT to be. That is not the same thing!

How have you labeled yourself something because of behavior?

_____
_____

Lord Jesus, what have I labeled myself, because of conned behavior that I was following, that has robbed me of my birthright as a child of God?

_____
_____
_____

Lord Jesus, help me understand and receive my new identity as Your child. I do not need to cling to regret or listen to the imposter anymore.

_____
_____

Lord Jesus, what am I missing out on because I am not "getting" this?

_____
_____
_____

Lord Jesus, where am I still asking You to pretty up my life instead of surrendering all of myself to You?

_____
_____

Lord, how do I need to forsake performance based acceptance, expectations over myself and others?

_____
_____
_____

Lord Jesus, help me see where I continue to operate from the Tree of the Knowledge of Good and Evil, rather than from Your Life. The Tree of Life is one of Your names.

_____
_____
_____

Lord, is there anything going on in my life, beliefs or knowledge, that is keeping me from the fullness of my new Life in You?

_____
_____
_____
_____
_____
_____
_____
_____
_____
_____
_____
_____
_____
_____
_____
_____
_____
_____
_____
_____

Trusting and Valuing God- Healer Sanctifier

What do you think about Donny's statement that Jesus still heals today?

_____
_____
_____

He Himself bore our sins in His body on the cross, so that we might die to sin and live to righteousness; for by His wounds you were healed. 2 Peter 2:24

†

For we are His workmanship, created in Christ Jesus for good works, which God prepared beforehand so that we would walk in them. Ephesians 2:10

†

Therefore if anyone is in Christ, he is a new creature; the old things passed away; behold, new things have come. 2 Corinthians 5:17

†

Such were some of you; but you were washed, but you were sanctified, but you were justified in the name of the Lord Jesus Christ and in the Spirit of our God. 1Corinthians 6:11

†

Now may the God of peace Himself sanctify you entirely; and may your spirit and soul and body be preserved complete, without blame at the coming of our Lord Jesus Christ. 1 Thessalonians 5:23

†

but like the Holy One who called you, be holy yourselves also in all your behavior; 16 because it is written, "You shall be holy, for I am holy." 1 Peter 1:15

Lord Jesus, how do I need to respond to You today?

_____
_____
_____

Lord Jesus, is there anything I need to let go of?

_____
_____
_____

Therefore He says: "God resists the proud, but gives grace to the humble."
James 4:6 (NKJV)

Lord, what do I need to let go of?

> Definition of Humble:
> Not proud (boastful) or arrogant.

_____
_____
_____

Lord, have I partnered with pride or self-sufficiency?

_____
_____

> This word, *proud*, has several meanings. The way Donny is using this word includes arrogance, or a feeling of superiority over others. This form of pride is boastful and rude.

What is the difference between "being perfect, as your Father in Heaven is perfect" and perfectionism?

_____
_____
_____

Would any of your relationships change if you could see those folks (or yourself) the way God sees them (or you)?

_____
_____

Partnering with God in relationship with others (and yourself) is possible and is our calling as believers.

Lord Jesus, is there something standing in the way of my partnership with You as You speak to those around me? I desire to be the expression of Your Life to my family, friends, and anyone You place in my life today. I give You permission to sharpen my awareness of Your mindset and to make it my own as well.
_____
_____

Lord Jesus, are You waiting on me?
_____
_____

Lord Jesus, am I trying to fix someone (myself or someone else) instead of trusting You with that person?
_____

Lord Jesus, have I partnered with pride or arrogance anywhere?
_____
_____
_____

Lord Jesus, do I need to forgive someone (F.E.D. Map) who taught me to partner with pride?
_____
_____
_____

Lord, what do I need to let go of?
_____
_____

Lord Jesus, if I were to give You my pride, what would You give me in exchange?

_____
_____
_____

Lord Jesus, I declare that You are my _____
and I am Your _____

Lord, thank you for being my Source of Life. Thank you that I cannot labor hard enough to manufacture what You have given me as a free gift. Lord, I give You permission to sharpen my awareness of Your perfection in my now. Amen.

Trusting and Valuing God – Need Meeter and Jealous Lover

Have you ever thought about God as your Need Meeter and Jealous Lover before? How does that sound/feel to you? True? Partly true? Never considered?
_____
_____
_____

Have you ever experienced a "dark night of the soul"?
_____
_____
_____

Do you feel like you can trust God with painful or scary circumstances?
_____
_____
_____

How do you feel about God when your need looks overwhelming? Like a financial crisis or a loved one who is dying.
_____
_____
_____

Do you feel like you are on your own in any area? If so, what area?
_____
_____
_____

But seek first His kingdom and His righteousness, and all these things will be added to you. Matthew 6:33

Matthew 6:1-23

"Beware of practicing your righteousness before men to be noticed by them; otherwise you have no reward with your Father who is in heaven.

"So when you give to the poor, do not sound a trumpet before you, as the hypocrites do in the synagogues and in the streets, so that they may be honored by men. Truly I say to you, they have their reward in full. But when you give to the poor, do not let your left hand know what your right hand is doing, so that your giving will be in secret; and your Father who sees what is done in secret will reward you.

"When you pray, you are not to be like the hypocrites; for they love to stand and pray in the synagogues and on the street corners so that they may be seen by men. Truly I say to you, they have their reward in full. But you, when you pray, go into your inner room, close your door and pray to your Father who is in secret, and your Father who sees what is done in secret will reward you.

"And when you are praying, do not use meaningless repetition as the Gentiles do, for they suppose that they will be heard for their many words. So do not be like them; for your Father knows what you need before you ask Him.

"Pray, then, in this way:

'Our Father who is in heaven,
Hallowed be Your name.
'Your kingdom come.
Your will be done,
On earth as it is in heaven.
'Give us this day our daily bread.
'And forgive us our debts, as we also have forgiven our debtors.
'And do not lead us into temptation, but deliver us from evil. [For Yours is the kingdom and the power and the glory forever. Amen.']

For if you forgive others for their transgressions, your heavenly Father will also forgive you. But if you do not forgive others, then your Father will not forgive your transgressions.

"Whenever you fast, do not put on a gloomy face as the hypocrites do, for they neglect their appearance so that they will be noticed by men when they are fasting. Truly I say to you, they have their reward in full. But you, when you fast, anoint your head and wash

your face so that your fasting will not be noticed by men, but by your Father who is in secret; and your Father who sees what is done in secret will reward you.

"Do not store up for yourselves treasures on earth, where moth and rust destroy, and where thieves break in and steal. But store up for yourselves treasures in heaven, where neither moth nor rust destroys, and where thieves do not break in or steal; for where your treasure is, there your heart will be also.

"The eye is the lamp of the body; so then if your eye is clear, your whole body will be full of light. But if your eye is bad, your whole body will be full of darkness. If then the light that is in you is darkness, how great is the darkness!

†

And my God will supply all your needs according to His riches in glory in Christ Jesus. Philippians 4:19

†

Hosea 2

Say to your brothers, "Ammi," and to your sisters, "Ruhamah."

"Contend with your mother, contend,

For she is not my wife, and I am not her husband;

And let her put away her harlotry from her face

And her adultery from between her breasts,

Or I will strip her naked

And expose her as on the day when she was born.

I will also make her like a wilderness,

Make her like desert land

And slay her with thirst.

"Also, I will have no compassion on her children,

Because they are children of harlotry.

"For their mother has played the harlot;

She who conceived them has acted shamefully.

For she said, 'I will go after my lovers,

Who give me my bread and my water,

My wool and my flax, my oil and my drink.'

"Therefore, behold, I will hedge up her way with thorns,

And I will build a wall against her so that she cannot find her paths.

"She will pursue her lovers, but she will not overtake them;

And she will seek them, but will not find them.

Then she will say, 'I will go back to my first husband,

For it was better for me then than now!'

"For she does not know that it was I who gave her the grain, the new wine and the oil,

And lavished on her silver and gold,

Which they used for Baal.

"Therefore, I will take back My grain at harvest time

And My new wine in its season.

I will also take away My wool and My flax

Given to cover her nakedness.

"And then I will uncover her lewdness

In the sight of her lovers,

And no one will rescue her out of My hand.

"I will also put an end to all her gaiety,

Her feasts, her new moons, her sabbaths

And all her festal assemblies.

"I will destroy her vines and fig trees,

Of which she said, 'These are my wages

Which my lovers have given me.'

And I will make them a forest,

And the beasts of the field will devour them.

"I will punish her for the days of the Baals

When she used to offer sacrifices to them

And adorn herself with her earrings and jewelry,

And follow her lovers, so that she forgot Me," declares the Lord.

"Therefore, behold, I will allure her,

Bring her into the wilderness

And speak kindly to her.

"Then I will give her her vineyards from there,

And the valley of Achor as a door of hope.

And she will sing there as in the days of her youth,

As in the day when she came up from the land of Egypt.

"It will come about in that day," declares the Lord,

"That you will call Me Ishi

And will no longer call Me Baali.

"For I will remove the names of the Baals from her mouth,

So that they will be mentioned by their names no more.

"In that day I will also make a covenant for them

With the beasts of the field,

The birds of the sky

And the creeping things of the ground.

And I will abolish the bow, the sword and war from the land,

And will make them lie down in safety.

"I will betroth you to Me forever;

Yes, I will betroth you to Me in righteousness and in justice,

In lovingkindness and in compassion,

And I will betroth you to Me in faithfulness.

Then you will know the Lord.

"It will come about in that day that I will respond," declares the Lord.

"I will respond to the heavens, and they will respond to the earth,

And the earth will respond to the grain, to the new wine and to the oil,

And they will respond to Jezreel.

"I will sow her for Myself in the land.

I will also have compassion on her who had not obtained compassion,

And I will say to those who were not My people,

'You are My people!'

And they will say, 'You are my God!'"

What do you think about Donny's assertion that idolatry is spiritual adultery?

_____
_____
_____

What happens in your soul when you consider God as the "Lover of your soul"? Does that sound plausible? What does that truth look or feel like in your now?

_____
_____
_____

Lord Jesus, am I seeing You rightly? Does my soul see You as my intimate Lover? Do I see You as the One who completes me?

_____
_____
_____

Lord Jesus, do I have intimacy issues with You?

_____
_____
_____

Lord, Jesus, do I have intimacy issues with others?
___
___
___

Lord Jesus, am I being an intimate lover with You?
___
___
___

Lord Jesus, have I been ignoring You in any area? Do we have a good connection?
___
___
___

Lord Jesus, I want to set aside special time with You each day. When would You like to do that?
___
___
___

Lord Jesus, do I need to forgive anyone for teaching me that You are difficult (or impossible) to connect with?
___
___
___

Revisit the F.E.D. Map if needed.

Trusting and Valuing God – Peacemaker

And the peace of God, which transcends all understanding, will guard your hearts and your minds in Christ Jesus. Philippians 4:7 (NIV)

†

Therefore, knowing the fear of the Lord, we persuade men, but we are made manifest to God; and I hope that we are made manifest also in your consciences. 12 We are not again commending ourselves to you but are giving you an occasion to be proud of us, so that you will have an answer for those who take pride in appearance and not in heart. 13 For if we are beside ourselves, it is for God; if we are of sound mind, it is for you. 14 For the love of Christ controls us, having concluded this, that one died for all, therefore all died; 15 and He died for all, so that they who live might no longer live for themselves, but for Him who died and rose again on their behalf.

16 Therefore from now on we recognize no one according to the flesh; even though we have known Christ according to the flesh, yet now we know Him in this way no longer. 17 Therefore if anyone is in Christ, he is a new creature; the old things passed away; behold, new things have come. 18 Now all these things are from God, who reconciled us to Himself through Christ and gave us the ministry of reconciliation, 19 namely, that God was in Christ reconciling the world to Himself, not counting their trespasses against them, and He has committed to us the word of reconciliation.

20 Therefore, we are ambassadors for Christ, as though God were making an appeal through us; we beg you on behalf of Christ, be reconciled to God. 21 He made Him who knew no sin to be sin on our behalf, so that we might become the righteousness of God in Him. 2 Corinthians 5:11 -21

Lord Jesus, am I resting in the Peace that I have with and in You?

_____
_____
_____

Lord Jesus, am I eager to make peace with others?

_____
_____
_____

Lord Jesus, am I at peace with myself? If not, why not?

_____
_____
_____

Remember to use the F.E.D. Map and the Emotional Compass when needed. The more you incorporate these crucial tools/skills into your now, the more natural or default they become. Your old default of flesh will actually give way to your new operating system of Grace! Putting off the old and putting on the new will happen less and less as you simply operate in the new in the now.

Therefore if you are presenting your offering at the altar, and there remember that your brother has something against you, 24 leave your offering there before the altar and go; first be reconciled to your brother, and then come and present your offering.
 Matthew 5:23,24

†

We are destroying speculations and every lofty thing raised up against the knowledge of God, and we are taking every thought captive to the obedience of Christ,
2 Corinthians 10:5

†

Be anxious for nothing, but in everything by prayer and supplication with thanksgiving let your requests be made known to God. 7 And the peace of God, which surpasses all comprehension, will guard your hearts and your minds in Christ Jesus.
Philippians 4:6,7

Lord Jesus, is there anything else You want me to know about Your Peace?

_____
_____
_____

Trusting and Valuing God – Lion & Lamb

...and one of the elders *said to me, "Stop weeping; behold, the Lion that is from the tribe of Judah, the Root of David, has overcome...Revelation 5:5

The next day he saw Jesus coming to him and said, "Behold, the Lamb of God who takes away the sin of the world! John 1:29

Lord Jesus, Thank You for the truth that, where I am weak, You are strong!

What happens in your soul as you consider Donny's assertion that you need both the Lion and the Lamb aspects of Christ's Life in order to navigate this world successfully and experience inner healing?

_____
_____
_____

Do you identify more with the Lion or the Lamb?

_____
_____
_____

Lord Jesus, am I holding on to unforgiveness towards someone who was more lion-ish or lamb-ish? Lord, is that person influencing me more than You are influencing me?

_____
_____
_____
_____
_____

Lord, do I have any unholy partnerships with the lion side or lamb side of me? Does my flesh show up as a lion or lamb?

_____
_____
_____

As a new creation in Christ, you are made in His image. Regardless of gender, you are His image bearer. What do you think about allowing Jesus to show you when be the Lion or Lamb?

_____
_____
_____

Lord Jesus, is there anything else You want me to know about the Lion and Lamb aspects of Life in You?

_____
_____
_____

Lord Jesus, show me how to make this truth a reality in my life.

_____
_____
_____
_____
_____
_____
_____
_____
_____

Trusting and Valuing God – Promise Keeper

Lord Jesus, am I still holding on to any broken promises (from me or from others)?
_____
_____
_____

The Lord will accomplish what concerns me; Your lovingkindness, O Lord, is everlasting; Do not forsake the works of Your hands. Psalm 138:8

Lord Jesus, what is it that You want to complete that concerns me?
_____
_____
_____

Lord, do I have my foot on the brake because of disappointments in my past?
_____
_____
_____

Lord Jesus, do I need to look over some verses and extend a deeper trust to You?
_____
_____
_____

Lord Jesus, how do I need to lean into You as my Promise Keeper?
_____
_____
_____
_____

Lord Jesus, if I give you my doubt or fear, what will You give me in exchange?

_____
_____
_____

Lord Jesus, how can I partner with You so that exchange is a reality in my life?

_____
_____
_____

Lord Jesus, have I judged You as a Promise Keeper? (Use the F.E.D. Map to expose the root and heal it)

_____
_____
_____

Lord Jesus, is there anything I need to give up in order to experience You more fully?

_____
_____
_____

Lord Jesus, do I question Your love for me? Do I doubt that You want and can provide the best for me?

_____
_____
_____

Lord Jesus, am I feeling entitled and expecting things that are not promised?

_____
_____

Lord Jesus, is there anything else You want me to know about Your role as my Promise Keeper?

Thoughts

Section Eight – Trusting and Valuing Others

Clover Tool

Mindset

Clover Tool Walk Through

Conflict and Communication "Drop the Rope"

C&C Identity Based Correction

Choose Your Path

PATH A: (Everyone)

Navigating Relationships in Abundance

Compass Intercessory Application

FED Intercessory Application

PATH B: (For Healthy Marriages)

T&V Others: Emotions

T&V Others: Finances

T&V Others: Roles

T&V Others: Spiritual

T&V Others: Recreation

T&V Others: Physical and Sexual

Journey Tools Wrap Up

Clover Tool

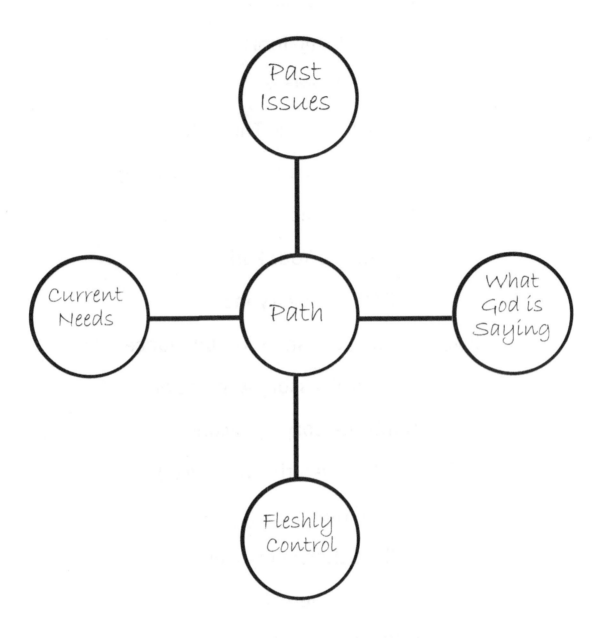

What stirs in your soul as you consider the Clover Tool?

_____
_____
_____

Clover Tool – Shift Mindset First

Mindset saturates everything you do.

I came that they may have life, and have it abundantly. John 10:10

Abundance	Scarcity
Victory in Christ	Victim
Healed	Wounded
Joyful	Bitter
Enough	Needy
Peace	Unrest/Disturbed/Anxious
Trusting	Striving/Trying
Purpose	Vanity/Futility
Pleased	Offended
Mercy	Judgement
Empowered	Shutdown/Trapped
Blameless/Justified	Guilty

For as he thinks in his heart, so is he. Psalm 23:7 (NLV)

†

Wealth adds many friends, but a poor man is separated from his friend. Proverbs 19:4

Lord Jesus, I give You permission to show me where I operate from a poverty mindset, rather than an Abundance mindset. Thank You for being my Enough. Is there any place where I think this way?

_____
_____
_____

The tongue has the power of life and death Proverbs 18:21 (NIV)

Lord, is there anything else You want me to know about my mindset?

_____
_____
_____

Lord Jesus, how can I partner with You to make Your Abundant Life a reality in my life? How can I understand more deeply the Truth that I am a partaker of Your Life?

_____
_____
_____
_____
_____
_____
_____
_____
_____
_____
_____
_____
_____

Clover Tool Walk Through

1. Check out the Word of God, by the Spirit of God for self-correction first.

2. Check your own mindset. If you are experiencing neediness, go to the Lord first so that you are operating from a place of abundance.

3. Listen to understand first, then seek to be understood. Use active listening.

4. Affirm and encourage the other person. Remind them of who they are in Christ.

5. Allow the Lord to connect and respond as He wills.

6. Ask, Lord, is now the right time for us to discuss this issue? Address neediness or woundedness through the F.E.D. Map or the Compasses.

7. If there is a flesh issue, affirm and use identity-based confrontation. Invite the other person to engage in exchange.

Finally, brethren, whatever is true, whatever is honorable, whatever is right, whatever is pure, whatever is lovely, whatever is of good repute, if there is any excellence and if anything worthy of praise, dwell on these things. Philippians 4:8

in everything give thanks; for this is God's will for you in Christ Jesus. 1Thessalonians 5:18

seeing that His divine power has granted to us everything pertaining to life and godliness, through the true knowledge of Him who called us by His own glory and excellence. 1 Peter 1:3

8. Engage in practical partnerships with each other and the Lord. Recreation, time spent, or fun activities.

9. Where might we need additional help from mentors, accountability partners, teachers, or counselors (relational healing).

10. What additional affirmation or reminders of Truth can you give yourself or the other? Try notes in a lunch box, or sticky-note on a mirror, or texting a sweet reminder of who they are.

11. Give thanks to God! He is up to something good. For you and for that other person!

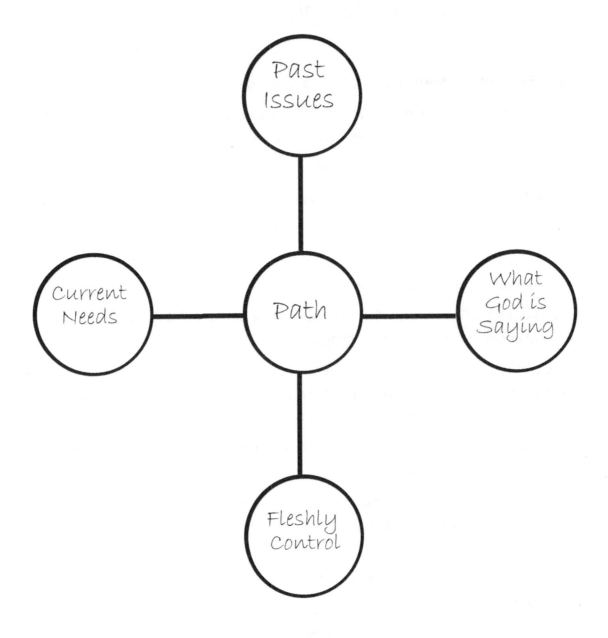

How can we practically partner with the Lord in all relational pathways?

Lord Jesus, where is this relationship in a deficit?

_____
_____

Trusting and Valuing Others – C&C Drop the Rope

… for the anger of man does not achieve the righteousness of God. James 1:20

What does it mean to "drop the rope"? What keeps me from dropping the rope when needed?
_____
_____
_____

Lord Jesus, is there someone I need to drop the rope with?
_____
_____

Thoughts

_____
_____
_____
_____
_____
_____
_____
_____
_____
_____
_____
_____
_____
_____
_____

Trusting and Valuing Others – C&C Identity Based Correction

Brethren, even if anyone is caught in any trespass, you who are spiritual, restore such a one in a spirit of gentleness; each one looking to yourself, so that you too will not be tempted. 2 Bear one another's burdens, and thereby fulfill the law of Christ.
Galatians 6:1,2 (NASB)

Lord Jesus, have I identified someone by their behavior? Have I judged someone who lied as a liar?

_____
_____
_____

Lord Jesus, have I identified or judged myself by my behavior?

_____
_____
_____

Lord Jesus, help me to see the person I am correcting as You see them. Help me encourage and equip them to overcome their negative behavior through Truth rather than through shame or blame.

Lord Jesus, is there anything else You want me to know about identity and identity based correction?

_____
_____
_____
_____
_____

Choose Your Path

PATH A: (Everyone)

Navigating Relationships in Abundance

Written by Robyn Henning

Let's continue our journey together as we look at some practical applications that Donny presented earlier in the section. All of us are in relationships whether we are single or married, divorced or widowed. Let's face it, relationships can be hard.

The key to effectively navigating relationships is _____.

It is from this mindset that we are entrusting ourselves, as Jesus did, to _____.

...and while being reviled, He did not revile in return; while suffering, He uttered no threats, but kept entrusting Himself to Him who judges righteously ... 1 Peter 2:23

When we entrust ourselves to Him we are at _____.

This is where we experience Him and the fullness of His love, joy and peace. Welcome to the abundant Life of Christ flowing in you and through you. Now maintaining this mindset moment by moment is the key to walking in victory.

Ask God how He wants you to set your mind in the morning so that you are tuned in to Him from the very beginning of the day. What has He shown you?

_____
_____
_____

In an earlier video, Donny recommended posting reminders where you will see them. What reminders have you posted?

As you are resting in Him and are aware of His presence, what worship songs or thoughts come from your heart to your mind?

Beloved, resting in His arms is the place of abundance that enables us to pour His abundance into the lives of those around us. He pours His agape love into us and through us.

What is agape?

When we choose to _____ to serve the _____ _____, no matter how _____; no matter _____.

That last part is the really hard part, but when we are living from _____ He empowers us respond with _____ instead of the _____ of our flesh.

The person that we are relating to cannot _____ of the life of Christ in us as long as we are _____ in Jesus.

So, beloved, no matter what the issue or the relationship, set your mind _____, and He will enable you to keep clear relational pathways with others.

<u>Thoughts</u>

_____
_____
_____
_____
_____
_____
_____
_____
_____
_____
_____

Compass Intercessory Application

CAUTION: The Spirit will not gossip or provide you this information if you are not pure in your motives. This is also not a word of knowledge that you share with the person that you are praying for or anyone else for that matter. This is for intercession only. He will not honor impure motives.

As the Spirit leads you on behalf of another roll through these questions:

"Lord what's _____ feeling right now? Answer: _____

"Lord, why's _____ feeling this way? Answer: _____

"Lord what else do You want me to know? Answer: _____

This is _____ prayer...like a laser targeted bomb dropped on the enemy's stronghold in their life.

Cycle through each compass if they apply, and ask the Spirit to show you on their behalf how to laser target your intercession for them.

Ask God who He wants you to intercede for using the compasses:

_____

_____

_____

FED Map Intercessory Application

CAUTION: The Spirit will not gossip or provide you this information if you are not pure in your motives. This is also not a word of knowledge that you share with the person that you are praying for or anyone else for that matter. This is for intercession only. He will not honor impure motives.

To target the enemy's strongholds in the other person's life, use the God Ask for them as you work through the FED Map grid:

"Lord Jesus, what lies about himself, God and others is _____ believing?"

"Lord Jesus, what labels has _____ owned about himself, God and others?"

"Lord Jesus what tools and strategies do You want _____ to be free from?"

"Lord Jesus, what vows has _____ made that need to be broken?"

You get the idea. Write down that the Lord shows you as you work through the FED map.

Once the Lord gives you His clear leading in how to intercede, here's how you approach the throne.

In Revelation 12:11 Satan is described as the _____.

He and his minions are like _____ standing before the Judge accusing us to Him.

Now, we know that all our sins are paid for in full and that this verdict has been rendered in heaven, but it is being worked out on earth in the sense that the battle still rages here.

Paul describes this battle as between our _____.

When we give into the _____ of the Flesh, we give the enemy _____ in our lives and _____ to accuse us with before the Lord.

The enemy seeks to keep us from walking in the _____ of Christ's life in us.

So, the goal of our intercession is to act as their _____ by pointing to _____ which has cleansed them from all iniquity.

When you intercede in this manner, you are coming into the throne room of God. Do so with the boldness spoken of in Hebrews 4:16, but it is to be done with the utmost reverence. This is not casual conversation with the Lord Jesus. (See 1 Timothy 2:1 and Psalm 20:5)

Here's an example:

"In the name of the Lord Jesus Christ, I humbly come before You based solely on the cleansing power of the Blood of the Lamb who has redeemed me and made me His child. I come before You on behalf of (person's name). He/She is under attack from the accuser of the brethren and his minions. But, _____ has accepted Jesus as his/her Savior and therefore, Satan has no legal claim to him/her or any ground in his/her life. In the name of the Lord Jesus Christ, I petition You to issue a decree against the forces of darkness commanding them to immediately cease their attack on him/her. I also petition You to issue a decree that reclaims all ground these spirits are claiming in _____'s life and to issue an eviction notice to them that goes into immediate effect. In the name of the Lord Jesus Christ, I thank You for hearing my petition. Amen."

This is laser-targeted prayer that will destroy enemy strongholds.

It is a privilege to come before the Righteous Judge with our petitions for others.

Ask God who He wants you to intercede for using the FED map:

_____

_____

_____

Thoughts

PATH B: (For Healthy Marriages)
Trusting and Valuing Others – Emotionally

Please note: the following material is designed for folks in healthy marriages. If you are in an abusive marriage, please ask God about how to process Path B. You are free to skip it altogether.

Check out Gary Chapman's great book called *The Five Love Languages*. Gary shares five different ways individuals receive and express love. Do you know your love language? Do you know your significant other's love language?

5 Love Languages

Words of Affirmation
Acts of Service
Receiving Gifts
Quality Time
Physical Touch

Lord Jesus, have I ever been wounded in a particular Love Language?

_____
_____
_____

If the answer is "yes", head back to the F.E.D. Map and get that healed.

What is the benefit to knowing the other person's Love Language?

_____
_____
_____

Nevertheless, each individual among you also is to love his own wife even as himself, and the wife must see to it that she respects her husband. Ephesians 5:33 (NASB)

†

If I speak with the tongues of men and of angels, but do not have love, I have become a noisy gong or a clanging cymbal. If I have the gift of prophecy, and know all mysteries and all knowledge; and if I have all faith, so as to remove mountains, but do not have love, I am nothing. And if I give all my possessions to feed the poor, and if I surrender my body to be burned, but do not have love, it profits me nothing.

Love is patient, love is kind and is not jealous; love does not brag and is not arrogant, does not act unbecomingly; it does not seek its own, is not provoked, does not take into account a wrong suffered, does not rejoice in unrighteousness, but rejoices with the truth; bears all things, believes all things, hopes all things, endures all things.

Love never fails; but if there are gifts of prophecy, they will be done away; if there are tongues, they will cease; if there is knowledge, it will be done away. For we know in part and we prophesy in part; but when the perfect comes, the partial will be done away. When I was a child, I used to speak like a child, think like a child, reason like a child; when I became a man, I did away with childish things. For now we see in a mirror dimly, but then face to face; now I know in part, but then I will know fully just as I also have been fully known. But now faith, hope, love, abide these three; but the greatest of these is love. 1 Corinthians 13 (NASB)

What happens in your soul when you consider unconditional respect? How might your relationship with your spouse, child, or friend change if you could see them for who they are. Every human is an eternal being and loved unconditionally by God.

_____
_____
_____

Lord Jesus, how can I express love and respect to _____
_____

Lord, is there anything else You want me to know about Love – especially Your Love?
_____
_____
_____
_____

Thoughts

Trusting and Valuing Others – Finances

Financial insecurities come from a poverty mindset or a poverty situation (or both).

Communicate in a shame-free, blame free-ways.

Remember this: Whoever sows sparingly will also reap sparingly, and whoever sows generously will also reap generously. Each of you should give what you have decided in your heart to give, not reluctantly or under compulsion, for God loves a cheerful giver.
2 Corinthians 9:6,7(NIV)

†

I came that they may have life and have it abundantly. John 10:10 (NASB)

Lord, how do You want me to engage with this _____?
_____
_____
_____

"Stewardship" reflects the character of the Master the steward serves.

A cheerful giver recognizes that he/she cannot out give God.

Lord Jesus, is there anything getting in the way of You giving me more?
_____
_____
_____

"No one can serve two masters; for either he will hate the one and love the other, or he will be devoted to one and despise the other. You cannot serve God and wealth.

"For this reason I say to you, do not be worried about your life, as to what you will eat or what you will drink; nor for your body, as to what you will put on. Is not life more than food, and the body more than clothing? Look at the birds of the air, that they do not

sow, nor reap nor gather into barns, and yet your heavenly Father feeds them. Are you not worth much more than they? And who of you by being worried can add a single hour to his life? And why are you worried about clothing? Observe how the lilies of the field grow; they do not toil nor do they spin, yet I say to you that not even Solomon in all his glory clothed himself like one of these. But if God so clothes the grass of the field, which is alive today and tomorrow is thrown into the furnace, will He not much more clothe you? You of little faith! Do not worry then, saying, 'What will we eat?' or 'What will we drink?' or 'What will we wear for clothing?' For the Gentiles eagerly seek all these things; for your heavenly Father knows that you need all these things. But seek first His kingdom and His righteousness, and all these things will be added to you. Matthew 6:24-33 (NASB)

†

"Whoever can be trusted with very little can also be trusted with much, and whoever is dishonest with very little will also be dishonest with much. Luke 16:10 (NIV)

Lord Jesus, thank You for the Abundant Life You desire me to experience and live from. Thank You that I cannot out give You! Please sharpen my awareness of poverty thinking. Help me understand how to live responsibly from my means, while not allowing my circumstance to define me.

I declare that You are my_____ and I am Your
_____

Lord Jesus, is there anything else You want me to know about partnering with You in the area of finances and stewardship?
_____
_____
_____

Lord Jesus, what can I do to make this Truth a reality in my life?
_____
_____

Trusting and Valuing Others – Roles

Traditional vs Modern roles are not as important as asking God what His desire is for your unique relationship.

Communication is key! Ask God for the right question to ask the other person.

Remember that you are a team! Expectations are often shaped by experience. Allow God to influence you more than your family of origin or previous relationships.

Resentment can be a great opportunity to walk through the Clover Tool. Pain is an indication of needed healing. Don't be afraid of conflict. Use conflict to increase oneness!

1. Check out the Word of God, by the Spirit of God for self-correction first.
2. Check your own mindset. If you are experiencing neediness, go to the Lord first so that you are operating from a place of abundance.
3. Listen to understand first, then seek to be understood. Use active listening.
4. Affirm and encourage the other person. Remind them of who they are in Christ.
5. Allow the Lord to connect and respond as He wills.
6. Ask, Lord, is now the right time for us to discuss this issue? Address neediness or woundedness through the F.E.D. Map or the Compasses.
7. If there is a flesh issue, affirm and use Identity Based Confrontation. Invite the other person to engage in exchange.
8. Engage in practical partnerships with each other and the Lord. Recreation, time spent, or fun activities.
9. Where might we need additional help from mentors, accountability partners, teachers, or counselors (relational healing).
10. What additional affirmation or reminders of Truth can you give yourself or the other? Try notes in a lunch box, or sticky-note on a mirror, or texting a sweet reminder of who they are.
11. Give thanks to God! He is up to something good. For you and for the other person!

Love each other through the expression of Godly roles and responsibilities. The roles of husband and wife, parent and child, friend to friend, these can all be shaped by our expectations and experiences. Allow God to be the One who shows you, teaches you, and guides you as you seek to express His love to that other person.

Lord, is there anything else You want me to know about my roles and responsibilities as a _____
_____
_____
_____

Lord, I give You permission to sharpen my awareness of my expectations for myself and others. I want to partner with You and be an expression of Your unconditional love and respect for _____

Lord, I declare that You are my _____ and I am Your _____.

Trusting and Valuing Others – Spiritual Growth

Oneness is an area where the enemy loves to attack.

As in everything, use the Clover Tool and Compasses as you discuss Spiritual growth with your spouse.

1. Check out the Word of God, by the Spirit of God for self-correction first.
2. Check your own mindset. If you are experiencing neediness, go to the Lord first so that you are operating from a place of abundance.
3. Listen to understand first, then seek to be understood. Use active listening.
4. Affirm and encourage the other person. Remind them of who they are in Christ.
5. Allow the Lord to connect and respond as He wills.
6. Ask, Lord, is now the right time for us to discuss this issue? Address neediness or woundedness through the F.E.D. Map or the Compasses.
7. If there is a flesh issue, affirm and use identity-based confrontation. Invite the other person to engage in exchange.
8. Engage in practical partnerships with each other and the Lord. Recreation, time spent, or fun activities.
9. Where might we need additional help from mentors, accountability partners, teachers, or counselors (relational healing).
10. What additional affirmation or reminders of Truth can you give yourself or the other? Try notes in a lunch box, or sticky-note on a mirror, or texting a sweet reminder of who they are.
11. Give thanks to God! He is up to something good. For you and for that other person!

Lord Jesus, is there anything else You would like me to know about Spiritual Growth and oneness with my spouse?

_____
_____
_____

Lord, I want to partner with You in this area of Spiritual growth. What can I do to make growth more of a reality in my life?

_____
_____
_____
_____
_____

Thoughts

Trusting and Valuing Others – Recreation

Fun! Do you remember having fun?

If you are married, keep dating your spouse. Keep having fun. Make your spouse's favorite activity something you do. Even if it's not your fave.

Sometimes having fun is a permission issue.

Lord Jesus, do I have permission to have fun? From You? From myself?

_____
_____
_____

Lord Jesus, why do I have my foot on the brake for having fun?

_____
_____
_____

If you have the brake on having fun, use the F.E.D. Map to forgive the person who taught you that having fun was not acceptable.

1. Check out the Word of God, by the Spirit of God for self-correction first.
2. Check your own mindset. If you are experiencing neediness, go to the Lord first so that you are operating from a place of abundance.
3. Listen to understand first, then seek to be understood. Use active listening.
4. Affirm and encourage the other person. Remind them of who they are in Christ.
5. Allow the Lord to connect and respond as He wills.
6. Ask, Lord, is now the right time for us to discuss this issue? Address neediness or woundedness through the F.E.D. Map or the Compasses.
7. If there is a flesh issue, affirm and use identity-based confrontation. Invite the other person to engage in exchange.
8. Where might we need additional help from mentors, accountability partners, teachers, or counselors (relational healing).

9. What additional affirmation or reminders of Truth can you give? What about a special movie that you know they would love, or dinner at their favorite restaurant?

10. Give thanks to God! He is up to something good. For you and for that other person!

Lord Jesus, how can I engage my spouse in fun ways? Lead me into creative ideas for recreation and fun. I know that You know him/her better than I do.

_____
_____
_____
_____

Lord, is there anything else You want me to know about having fun?

_____
_____
_____
_____

Lord, I want to partner with You in fun ways that enrich and encourage my relationship with _____. I give You permission to prompt me in ways I may not be accustomed to.

Thoughts

_____
_____
_____
_____
_____
_____
_____
_____

Trusting and Valuing Others – Physical and Sexual Intimacy

How does your soul respond/react to Donny's assertion that "any problem in the marriage will show up in the bedroom"?

_____
_____
_____

Sexual intimacy may seem difficult to discuss with your spouse, but God is able and desires to enrich your marriage in this way.

How does your soul respond/react to Donny's comment about rejection?

_____
_____
_____

Has your spouse rejected you sexually? Have you rejected your spouse? Do you know why?

_____
_____
_____
_____

Real healing is possible, ask the Lord if past rejection is part of your present pain if you struggle with either being rejected, or rejecting the other.

The wife does not have authority over her own body, but the husband does; and likewise also the husband does not have authority over his own body, but the wife does. Stop depriving one another, except by agreement for a time, so that you may devote yourselves to prayer, and come together again so that Satan will not tempt you because of your lack of self-control. 1 Corinthians 7:4,5

Use the Clover Tool to guide communication about your union, oneness and intimacy.

1. Check out the Word of God, by the Spirit of God for self-correction first.
2. Check your own mindset. If you are experiencing neediness, go to the Lord first so that you are operating from a place of abundance.
3. Listen to understand first, then seek to be understood. Use active listening.
4. Affirm and encourage the other person. Remind them of who they are in Christ.
5. Allow the Lord to connect and respond as He wills.
6. Ask, Lord, is now the right time for us to discuss this issue? Address neediness or woundedness through the F.E.D. Map or the Compasses.
7. If there is a flesh issue, affirm and use identity-based confrontation. Invite the other person to engage in exchange.
8. Engage in practical partnerships with each other and the Lord.
9. Where might we need additional help from mentors, accountability partners, teachers, or counselors (relational healing).
10. What additional affirmation or reminders of Truth can you give the other? Try sending flowers to her workplace, or a card to his. Remind them of who they are.
11. Give thanks to God! He is up to something good. For you and for your other!

Come up with a secret non-verbal way to communicate interest, if that seems fun.

Lord Jesus, do I have any pain or wounding regarding sex?
_____
_____
_____

Lord Jesus, is there anything else You want me to know about intimacy with my spouse?
_____
_____
_____

Journey Tools Wrap Up

We trust that this has been an amazing journey for you. Remember we are here for you. Ask God what His next steps are for you. We encourage you to go back through the videos with your workbook and engage the Lord some more to ferret out any lingering issues.

He is going to nudge some of you toward group facilitator training. If that's what He's doing, don't hesitate. Contact your group facilitator to discuss the Journey Tools Group Facilitator training program.

Also, we love testimonies! Please ask God if he wants you to put your testimony on video to encourage others. Who doesn't love a testimony of God's amazing grace at work!

Lastly, invite your friends and everyone else for that matter. We all need healing, and we serve Jehovah Rapha, the God who heals. God bless you!

Thank you for joining us on this Journey!

Section Nine - Blank Forms/Resources*

F.E.D. Map

5 Stages of Grief

God Ask/Triangle Tool

*All of these materials are copyrighted and represent a lifetime of work. Please respect and protect Donny's intellectual property by using these forms for yourself only.

Deep Cleaning FED Map

Overt Action/Event: _____ Done by: _____ DIY/DIW: _____

Rate the pain: _____ (1–10) When to Process _____ Ability to Forgive _____ (1-10)

	LIE	LABEL	TOOL/STRATEGY	VOW	NEEDS	EMOTIONS
Myself						
Exchange						
God						
Exchange						
Role of Offender						
Exchange						
Role of Recipient						
Exchange						
Action/Object Used						
Exchange						
Anything Else						
Exchange						

5 Stages of Recovery & Life Transition

Stage:	Description:	Permission:	Crisis of:	Choice Between:

5 Stages of Recovery & Life Transition

Stage:	Description:	Permission:	Crisis of:	Choice Between:
Denial	"There's no problem!" "What problem?" "Stop telling me I have a problem!"	To see and feel the problem	Reality	Insanity or Hope
Anger	Emotionally explosive or implosive blame	Forgive and let go	Judgement and Justice	Remaining burdened or feeling lighter
Bargaining	Testing God, self and others (how close can I get w/o getting burned?)	Try Fail Succeed	Boundaries	Holding on the old patterns or mapping out new paths
Depression	Focused on circumstance, losses, external world, overwhelming pressure	Live without fear (financial, loved one,)	Worth — Am I worth loving even if I can't ____? Are the false promises worth pursuing?	Giving in to external limits/labels of others or receiving God's limitless love
Acceptance	Authentic Peace	Accept the true nature of God, identity in Christ, ourselves, and our supply	Presence and peace	Playing games with who I am, listening to the enemy or remembering that God supplies ALL my need in Christ

The God Ask

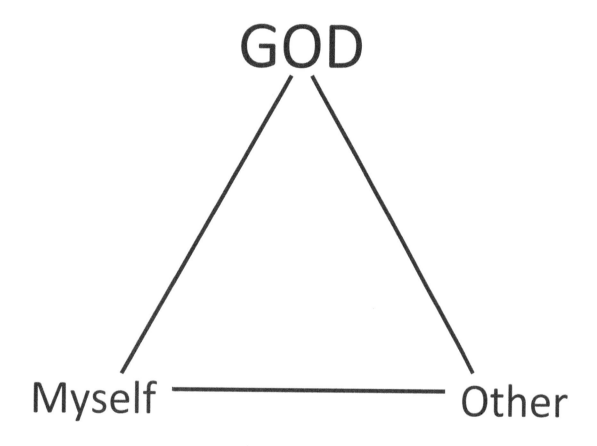

Made in the USA
Middletown, DE
07 March 2025